Lectionary Stories
Cycle C

40 Tellable Tales for Advent, Christmas, Epiphany, Lent, Easter and Pentecost

By John E. Sumwalt

C.S.S. Publishing Co.
Lima, Ohio

All characters and stories in this book are fictitious except for those in the chapters titled "Rapture," "An Old Enemy," "Source Of Comfort," "A Fist And A Kiss," "Praying To Win," "Jerry's Faith" and "The Red Mules."

Scripture quotations are from the New Revised Standard Version of the Bible, copyright 1989 by the Division of Christian Education of the National Council of the Churches of Christ in the USA. Used by permission.

Library of Congress Cataloging-in-Publication Data

Sumwalt, John E.
    Lectionary stories. Cycle C : 40 tellable stories for Advent,
Christmas, Epiphany, Lent, Easter, and Pentecost / by John E.
Sumwalt.
        p.   cm.
    ISBN 1-55673-324-0
    1. Homiletical illustrations.   2. Common lectionary.   3. Bible —
Homiletical use.   I. Title.   II. Title: 40 tellable stories for
Advent, Christmas, Epiphany, Lent, Easter, and Pentecost.
III. Title: Forty tellable stories for Advent, Christmas, Epiphany,
Lent, Easter, and Pentecost
BV4225.2.S956   1991
251'.08—dc20   91-18574
                                                                   CIP

9148 / ISBN 1-55673-324-0   PRINTED IN U.S.A.

In loving memory
of Donald E. Sumwalt

Acknowledgements

My thanks to Richard Steele and Jo Perry-Sumwalt for critiquing the manuscript — and to Wesley White, Dale Hanaman, Joe Amico, Steven Savides, Jim Hachten-Cotter, Ruby and Bill Dow for critiquing selected stories.

My special thanks to Joyce Alford for her encouragement and support — and to the congregations of Trinity United Methodist Church in Montello, Cargill United Methodist Church in Janesville, and Wesley United Methodist Church in Kenosha who have both suffered and rejoiced with me in the birthing of these stories.

To my storytelling friends, Lloyd Lewis, Bob Hays, Charles Logsdon Christopher, Owen Miller and Michael Williams, thanks for the inspiration.

Contents

A Call To Stories

Storytelling is fundamental to the human search for meaning . . .[1]

Mary Catherine Bateson

After every call to arms there follows a call to stories. The sorting out — the understanding of the meaning of a war, a victory or a defeat, the suffering and the death — goes on for generations after the last battle has been fought. All of the survivors — the soldiers and the civilians on both sides, the wounded, the refugees, the returned POWs, the bereaved soul whose loved one was killed and the joyful heart whose love came safely home — have stories to tell, stories which must be told and heard if they are to be whole again. The telling and retelling of these stories will shape the beliefs, the fears and the hopes of generations to come.

For those of us who tell stories for the community from pulpits, the stage, the movie screen, in classrooms or board rooms, this is a time for prayerful listening. We must listen as if our very lives and the lives of every living soul depend on it — because they do! If we listen well to the wounded, the dying and the bereaved victims of war, we will with God's help be able to tell stories that make a redemptive difference in the lives of those who hear them. The world has never had a greater need for healing, saving, life-giving stories than in these latter days of the war-weary 20th century.

I am grateful to Kendall Anderson of Turtle Lake, Wisconsin, and Kenneth Morgan of Princeton, New Jersey, for sharing personal stories of conflicts past *(An Old Enemy,* p. 28; *A Source Of Comfort,* p. 30 and *A Fist And A Kiss,* p. 72) which I believe will give inspiration and hope to all who are committed to the hard work of loving and healing that will go on for years after the Persian Gulf war has ended.

These Stories Are For Telling

You have my permission to tell these stories as your own. There is no need to mention my name or the title of the book, unless of course someone should come up to you after the telling with checkbook in hand and ask where the stories can be found. If in the course of sharing one of these tales a crowd should turn on you and chase you out of a synagogue or church, do not pause to mention my name — appeal to the one who is the giver of all stories.

[1]Mary Catherine Bateson, *Composing A Life,* (The Atlantic Monthly Press, 1989), p. 34.

Apocalypse Child

Be alert at all times, praying that you may have the
strength to escape all these things that will take place,
and to stand before the Son of Man.

Luke 21:36

While other children were watching cartoons and playing in backyard sandboxes, Scotty was drilling his soldiers and watching Headline News. He would do nothing else. His grandparents pleaded with him to go outside and play with the other children. "You need fresh air and sunshine," they told him. But he wouldn't go. "I have to be ready," he said. Day after day he drilled and watched.

Then one day he saw them, his mom and dad, dressed in desert uniforms and looking out at him from the television screen. "We have a son at home," they told the reporter. "Hi, Scotty," they called out over the airwaves. "We love you. We'll be home soon." Scotty waved at them and they waved back. His mom threw him a kiss and his dad saluted. And then the picture faded and Scotty went outside to play.

A Voice Crying In The Wilderness

. . . the word of God came to John, son of Zechariah, in the wilderness. He went into all the region around the Jordan, proclaiming a baptism of repentance for the forgiveness of sins, as it is written in the book of the words of the prophet Isaiah, "The voice of one crying out in the wilderness: Prepare the way of the Lord . . . ."

Luke 3:2b-4b

"I'm expecting," an old woman announced to a visitor one day. She was strapped in a wheelchair and a bib was tied around her neck. "The baby is coming any day now," she said, patting her midsection.

"Pay no attention to her," an aide told the visitor, as she moved to wheel the old woman back to her room, "she says that all the time. Shame on you Lucille, you are no more expecting than the man in the moon. Why don't you stop all this silly talk?"

"I am too expecting," Lucille insisted, "the doctor told me I am."

That was the day Cindy began working in the nursing home and about three months before she learned that she was pregnant. By that time she and Lucille had become fast friends. Cindy worked in housekeeping, so she got into all of the residents' rooms every day. She visited with each one as she cleaned. Lucille soon became her favorite. Aside from her imaginary pregnancy she seemed very much in touch with the real world, and she was a delightful conversationalist. She had been a hairdresser before she retired, and so had much to tell about all the people who had come into her shop over the years.

As Cindy began to show she and Lucille talked more and more about babies. Lucille had never had a child of her own. "This would be her first," she said. Cindy never knew quite what to say when she came out with things like that. She didn't encourage her but she didn't argue with her either.

Each day when Cindy came to work, Lucille would ask her how she was feeling and what the baby had been doing. Cindy would tell her about the baby's kicking and somersaults and hiccups. Sometimes, when the baby was especially active she would allow Lucille to put her hand on her stomach and feel the baby's movements.

A few weeks after the baby was born Cindy brought him to the nursing home to show everyone. She took him to Lucille's room first and triumphantly handed him into Lucille's waiting arms. Lucille cuddled him for a while, asked his name and insisted that Cindy tell her all about the delivery. When she was finished telling all that she could remember, Cindy asked Lucille if she would like to hold the baby as she showed him around. Lucille beamed with delight.

"He's here, He's here! The baby's here," Lucille called out as Cindy wheeled them down the hallway. Everyone stopped what they were doing and hurried over to see the baby. "He's here at last," Lucille told them, "And his name is Joshua."

Judgment Day

John answered all of them by saying, "I baptize you with water; but one who is more powerful than I is coming; I am not worthy to untie the thong of his sandals. He will baptize you with the Holy Spirit and with fire. His winnowing fork is in his hand, to clear his threshing floor and to gather the wheat into his granary; but the chaff he will burn with un-quenchable fire."

Luke 3:16-17

The small boy was often seen down by the lake with his cane pole. Every evening, just before the supper hour, he would pass by the store fronts in the town with his catch of the day. Sometimes there would be a bass or a northern pike, but usually it was a big carp or a string of suckers. His mother, who re-lied on the fish to supplement the groceries she was able to buy with their family's allotment of foodstamps, was glad for whatever he brought. Filleted, soaked overnight in salt water, fried in beer batter or baked in butter and cornmeal, they tasted as good as trout in the finest restaurant.

It was mid-July when the chamber of commerce announced that it was time to seine the rough fish out of the lake. The tourists were beginning to complain that they weren't catch-ing enough game fish. Something had to be done before they went elsewhere to fish and spend their tourist dollars. Seining day was set for August 1, a Saturday when all the men would be free to help. The dam was opened a few days before, so that the water level would be low, allowing easy access to the fish. They started early in the morning, about 30 men with a dozen boats and nets they had borrowed from the Depart-ment of Natural Resources. By evening almost 9,000 pounds

14

of rough fish, carp, redhorse and suckers had been removed from the 45-acre lake and packed into hundred pound boxes for shipment to a fertilizer company in Des Moines. A much smaller amount of game fish, northern pike, large mouth bass, blue gills and crappies, were thrown back. Now there would be good fishing for the tourists.

Late that night the small boy got an old bucket from under the porch and dipped it into a milk tank behind the shed in the back yard. The tank was swimming full of carp, redhorse and suckers. He filled his pail with water and fish and carried it through the town and down to the lake. Before the sun came up he had made over a dozen trips, stopping only to watch as the fish made their way through the shallows to the deep.

The next day he was back at the lake with his cane pole, fishing in his usual spot.

Author's Note: *Alternate Text, Matthew 13:24-30, The Parable Of The Weeds.*

The Virgin Maude

In those days Mary set out and went with haste to a Judean town in the hill country, where she entered the house of Zechariah and greeted Elizabeth. When Elizabeth heard Mary's greeting, the child leaped in her womb. And Elizabeth was filled with the Holy Spirit and exclaimed with a loud cry, "Blessed are you among women, and blessed is the fruit of your womb."

Luke 1:39-42

Emily was in a hurry to be done with her visiting. There was just one last call to be made and then she could take her maternity leave and forget about her pastoral duties for a while. She entered the old woman's room somewhat hesitantly. She never knew quite what to expect from Maude Brown. Maude had never known a "woman preacher," as she called Emily, in all of her 98 years. And she made it very clear that she didn't like the idea one bit. She would never call Emily "Reverend" or "Pastor." It was always "Mrs. Sheldon."

As Emily approached the bed, the old woman raised her head and struggled to make out who she was. "It's Emily, Miss Brown, Emily Sheldon, your pastor from the church. How are you today?"

"Why I'm just fine for an old woman. And how are you, Mrs. Sheldon? You look like you need to sit down and take a load off your feet. You shouldn't be out running around in your condition. You should be home with your husband. Let him do the running."

Emily sat down, and as she sat she felt the baby leap in her womb. Maude saw her wince and reach for her stomach. She asked Emily if she would allow her to feel the baby.

Emily was a little taken aback. This was the first time this had ever happened to her during a pastoral visit. But she told Maude to go ahead. It would be perfectly all right.

Emily pulled her chair over closer to the bed. Maude stretched out a wrinkled hand and placed it gently on her swollen middle. The two women waited in silence until the baby stirred again. Maude sighed and removed her hand. The silence continued for several moments. Then, in a low voice and with eyes looking off into the distance, Maude began to speak.

"I was expecting once. It happened when I was very young. The hired man had his way with me in the haymow one day when Mama and Papa were gone. He made me promise not to tell them. When I started to get big about three months later, Mama said, 'Girl, what are we going to do with you?' She didn't ask me who or why. She didn't even get angry with me. She simply said, 'Maude, you must ride the horse every day for a half hour.' I didn't much like riding the horse, but I didn't argue with her. Mama watched me closely after that but it wasn't until about two weeks later that the bleeding started. Mama put me in bed and told me to push until it was all out. She took it away. I don't know what she did with it. We never spoke of it, and I never rode the horse again."

Emily reached out and took hold of Maude's hand. "It's okay," she said. "I'm glad you told me. May I sit with you for little while? We don't have to talk if you don't want to."

"I'd like that," Maude said.

When Emily got up to leave about a hour later, Maude opened her eyes and said, "Thank you, Reverend, I'm glad you came."

This Will Be A Sign

This will be a sign for you: you will find a child wrapped in bands of cloth and lying in a manger.
                                                      Luke 2:12

Christ Church put on a live nativity every year about two weeks before Christmas. They had the perfect location downtown on the square across from the clock tower. Everyone who drove into the business district went right by the front lawn of the church. There were slums, and street people who slept in the park a few blocks away, but you couldn't see them from the church. They set the nativity up on the lawn on the designated evening after dark and flooded it with carefully placed spotlights. For anyone driving around the square it was a dazzling sight, a Christmas card come to life. When word got out people came from miles around, from all over the city and the suburbs.

At first it was just a few bales of hay stacked up to give some semblance of a stable, a couple of sheep and two sets of parents with small babies who took turns portraying the holy family. But as the crowds grew each year the nativity became a bigger and bigger production with shepherds, wise men, an inn keeper, King Herod, a small flock of sheep with lambs for the children to pet, a donkey for Mary to ride, cows with calves, chickens, ducks, geese, and, thanks to special arrangements made through the local Shriners, three genuine two-hump camels to carry the wise men as they followed the star. The star rolled along on a track which had been laid out across the roof line of the church. They rented doves one year to perch on top of the stable and coo, but they couldn't get them to coo on cue and they discovered that the pigeons that flew down from the clock tower could play the part just as well, and they were free, so that was the end of rented doves.

18

The latest addition had been a 40-voice angel choir with the choir director Tom Grover playing the part of the archangel Gabriel. Tom loved to dress up in his flowing white robes and magnificent wings with gold glitter on the tips. He suggested that he carry a flaming sword when he made the announcement to the shepherds, but the director thought that would be too much. They did give him a special halo with soft blue light which made him stand out from the others whose halos were a much dimmer white. One of the guys in the tenor section said he looked like he was announcing a K-Mart special.

The angel choir sang from an elevated stage erected on the far edge of the lawn in front of the church's three large air conditioning units. Surrounded by clouds painted on cardboard, and raised and lowered hydraulically, it made for a wonderful dramatic moment when their lights came on and they appeared out of the darkness singing "It Came Upon The Midnight Clear." For the grand finale at the end of each half-hour performance they formed themselves into a giant living Christmas tree and sang "Joy To The World."

One year, at their late summer planning meeting, the director announced that they needed a sign, a big billboard somewhere downtown, perhaps visible from the freeway, with a picture of the nativity and an invitation for everyone to come and see it at Christ Church. He said it would be a good way of expanding their ministry and it would be great publicity for the church. The senior pastor said that she knew a retired sign painter in the congregation and offered to ask him to paint the sign. Someone else offered to make arrangements to rent a billboard and to talk to some of the wealthy members about paying for it. Everyone thought it was a wonderful idea.

At their next meeting in mid-October it was reported that plans were well under way and the sign would be ready just after Thanksgiving. The retired sign painter had responded with great enthusiasm to the idea of painting the nativity on a billboard for all of the city to see. He said it had been a life-long dream to paint a sign that would be a witness to his faith. He had asked for only one consideration — "a free hand in

19

painting the nativity as the Holy Spirit led," was the way he put it. And they were glad to agree. They had seen his work and they knew there was no one better in the sign painting business. No one was to see the sign until the unveiling on the first Sunday of Advent.

There were several more meetings after that. As Advent approached there was an air of excitement in the church like they had never experienced before. When word got around about the billboard everyone wanted to be in the nativity. They had to create several more roles: shepherd boys and shepherd girls, the innkeeper was to have children hanging on his arm this year and a wife doing chores in the background, there would be a dozen more angels and the wise men would have servants following along behind the camels. They rented several more animals including a goat and a flock of peacocks. It would add more atmosphere, they said.

The unveiling was scheduled for noon, after the last worship service, on the first Sunday of Advent. The church was packed and, after the benediction, the choir, dressed in their nativity costumes, led the whole congregation out the door, around the square and down a couple of blocks to where the billboard was located near the downtown off ramp next to the freeway. It was one of the best advertising locations in the city. Two hundred thousand people would see the sign every week.

The mayor of the city was to assist the pastor and the nativity director in the unveiling. The retired sign painter was standing by. It would be his moment of triumph. A newspaper photographer was to take his picture standing in front of the sign after it was unveiled. One of the television stations had sent a reporter and a camera crew, and of course, several people in the congregation had brought video cameras. Every one had a sense that this was to be an historic moment.

The ceremonies started with a brief speech by the nativity director, followed by a few words of greeting from the mayor and a prayer of consecration led by the pastor. Then came the moment they had all been waiting for. The choir began to sing "Away In A Manger" softly in the background. The director signaled for the cloth that was covering the sign to be raised. They all craned their necks upwards and waited. And then they saw it. At first there was a kind of quiet murmur that rippled through the crowd, then gasps, followed by a din of wonderment which grew into what sounded like a roar of disapproval. They couldn't believe what they were seeing! It looked nothing at all like their beautiful nativity. The sign painter had painted a simple cardboard shack with a contemporary Joseph and Mary who looked very much like the street people who lived in the park a few blocks from the church. Baby Jesus was wrapped in rags and lying in a tattered disposable diaper box. There were no shepherds or wisemen, no angels with gold-tipped wings. There was only a bag lady and a cop who had come by on his horse. They were both kneeling in front of the diaper box and the babe appeared to be smiling at them. Underneath the picture were painted the words:

This will be a sign for you:
you will find a child wrapped
in bands of cloth and lying
in a manger.

They put the best face on things that they could. The director said something about the church's ministry to the poor. What else were they going to say? They couldn't say that it was a mistake on live television, in front of the mayor and the whole city. But it was difficult to hide their disappointment. Everyone was gone within five minutes of the unveiling. The retired sign painter was left alone with the television reporter to try to explain his modern rendering of the nativity. But even he was beginning to wonder if he had made a mistake. His wife, his children and his grandchildren had left with everyone else. He wondered if they would ever forgive him for this embarrassment to the family. Perhaps they would never go to church with him again.

It was on Monday morning, just after the church secretary came to work, about eight o'clock, that the phone started to ring. There were not only calls from within the city, there were calls from all over the country — newspaper reporters, disc jockeys, talk show hosts; everyone wanted to hear more about the sign. And the calls kept coming all week. Soon everyone in the nation knew about Christ Church's unusual sign. The retired sign painter became an overnight celebrity. By Thursday he had been on two national talk shows and was scheduled for Oprah the next week.

The following Sunday the church was filled to overflowing at both services. The pastor was so taken aback that by the second service she had discarded her prepared notes and was talking about the miracle that God had worked among them. She suggested that while the nativity was a wonderful ministry, perhaps God was calling them to a new ministry with the poor and homeless. Perhaps they could start a shelter in the basement of the church and maybe they could help the Habitat folks build and renovate houses in the slums of their city. When she was finished preaching, the choir sang "Joy To The World" as they led the congregation out the door, around the square, and down the two blocks to the sign. There they stopped and looked again at the child who smiled out at them from the rags and cardboard shack.

From somewhere near the front of the congregation there came the soft sound of a single voice. It was Tom Grover, the choir director, and he was singing:

> *What child is this who laid to rest,*
> *on Mary's lap is sleeping?*
> *Whom angels greet with anthems sweet,*
> *while shepherds watch are keeping?*

And then the choir and the whole congregation joined with him, singing with all of their might:

This, this is Christ the King,
whom shepherds guard and angels sing;
haste, haste to bring him laud,
the babe, the son of Mary.

William C. Dix, "What Child Is This," *The United Methodist Hymnal,* (Nashville, The United Methodist Publishing House, 1989), p. 219.

Beautiful Feet

*How beautiful upon the mountains are the feet of
the messenger who announces peace, who brings
good news, who announces salvation . . .*

Isaiah 52:7a

Earl Bentner had beautiful feet. They were big, too. It was
the first thing people noticed about him when he was a baby.
"Look at those feet," they would say. "He's going to wear
size 16 shoes." And then, of course, they wanted to touch
them. Baby Earl got very tired of people pulling at his toes.

It became worse as Earl grew older. His feet not only got
bigger, they became more and more beautiful. They were his
most noticeable feature, like some people have stick-out ears
or a prominent nose, Earl had big, beautiful feet. There was
just something about them. No one could resist those long,
delicate toes and supple arches — and heels that were a study
in physiological perfection. People noticed them and
commented on them like they would comment on the hands
of a fine pianist. They were, well, beautiful.

But they were also a constant source of embarrassment to
Earl, especially during those awkward teenage years. Everywhere he went people would say, "Show us your feet Earl."
It didn't matter whether it was winter or summer. And Earl
would always oblige, but inside he felt like some kind of freak,
and he began to harbor feelings of resentment, although he
did kind of enjoy it when the girls caressed his arches.

He became something of a celebrity. The local newspaper
ran a front page article one year. Pictures of Earl's feet were
seen all over the country. Earl revelled in all the attention at
first but after a while the resentment returned and he began
to wish that he had been born with ordinary feet.

24

The low point in Earl's life occurred when he failed his army physical. The year was 1941. Earl had just graduated from high school. The whole country was gearing up for the war. Earl and several of his classmates received their draft notices at the same time. They were all excited as they rode the bus into the city. They talked about sticking together after boot camp. Every one passed the physical but Earl. The doctor took one look at his feet and said, "Too big. The army doesn't have any shoes that big." He wrote something in red on the bottom of Earl's form and told him to go home.

Earl moped around for several weeks before he decided that what he needed to do was to get out of town and find some kind of work. He took a job at a saw mill in a small village up in the mountains. It was hard work, but it helped him forget about his disappointment and nobody paid any attention to his feet. He just happened to be in the village store on that Saturday evening, December 6, when the mountain was hit with one of the worst blizzards that any one could remember. He and several other men from the mill were stranded there all night. The snow was so deep on the road and the winds so fierce that there was no way that any of them could have left the store. The storm was still raging the next morning when the word came about the attack on Pearl Harbor. They all huddled around the radio and listened in horror as the announcer described the utter devastation inflicted on the U.S. fleet by the Japanese bombers. The picture grew worse and worse as the reports kept coming in all day long. More than 2,000 U.S. military personnel killed, 80 naval aircraft and 97 army planes destroyed and 19 ships sunk, including the battleships West Virginia, Oklahoma, Utah and Arizona.

"Isn't Jimmy Everson on the Arizona?" It was old Burt Meeker, the owner of the store who spoke. "Yep, I believe he is," he said, answering his own question. "His brother Jack is in the army down at Fort Dix, but I remember their dad saying that Jimmy was on the Arizona over in Pearl. Sam and Edith must be worried sick."

It was two days later when the store phone rang, the only phone on the mountain. Everyone was still there. The blizzard had stopped, but the snow was 15 feet deep and the county crews had only begun to clear the roads. The conversation stopped as Burt picked up the phone. When he hung up they knew from what they had been able to hear of his side of the conversation that Jimmy Everson was all right and he wanted them to get word to his folks.

"I'll go," Earl said immediately. "Lend me your snow shoes, Burt, and I'll follow the road."

"No you won't," Burt declared. "It's more than two miles up to the Everson place. If that wind comes up again you would be lost in five minutes."

"I have to go. I know how my folks would feel if it was me that was on that ship."

They all tried to talk him out of it, but he wouldn't listen. About two hours later, and only a half mile up the road, he wished that he had. The harder the wind blew, the more difficult it became to follow the road. Something made him keep going. At the end of the sixth hour it was beginning to get dark and he was nearly exhausted. He wanted to lie down in the snow and rest for a while, but he knew enough to keep himself moving. Then, suddenly, there was a light in front of him and he heard a voice calling out over the wind, "Over here." He struggled toward the light and the voice. Sam and Edith Everson caught him as he stumbled onto the porch. They helped him onto a stool by the door and waited for him to catch his breath. Earl could see the fear that was in their eyes. Would it be good news or bad? As soon as he was able to speak, he blurted out the words they had been waiting to hear, "Jimmy called. He's okay."

Edith burst into tears and Sam grabbed a hold of her and hugged her tight. Then they went after Earl. He thought Edith never was going to stop kissing him.

"Why are we standing out here in the cold? Come on inside," Sam said. "Come over here and warm yourself by the fire. Make yourself at home. Put your feet up."

An Old Enemy

Bear with one another and, if any one has a complaint against another, forgive each other; just as the Lord has forgiven you, so you also must forgive. Above all clothe yourselves with love, which binds everything together in perfect harmony.
Colossians 3:13-14

We met on a commercial flight between Minneapolis and Detroit sometime in the late 1950s. He was Oriental. It was almost 15 years after the war. I don't remember his name, but I still have his business card somewhere in my desk. I'm not sure why I sat beside him. In those days the airlines still allowed you to pick your own seat. I could have sat with any number of people, or I could have sat by myself. For some reason I chose to sit beside him.

The plane took off, and after we had been flying for a little while I asked him if he was Japanese. He said yes. On an impulse I decided to tell him a story that I had just heard — about a man who died and was given the option of going to heaven or hell. He decided to go to hell because he thought that was where his friends were most likely to be. When he arrived in hell he discovered that there was plenty of rice and other good things to eat, but everyone was starving because the chopsticks were all six feet long. He didn't like the looks of things in hell, so he asked if he could go to heaven instead. He was given permission to go and when he arrived he discovered that everything was exactly the same, except in heaven they were feeding each other.

"Oh," my companion said, "you must be a Christian. I am too."

He went on to tell that his mother was a Christian and that he had become a Christian after the war. I asked him what he had done during the war. He said that he had been a fighter pilot in the Southwest Pacific. I told him that I had been a fighter pilot too, in the same area. We quickly compared notes and discovered that we had flown missions over Formosa at the same time. Neither of us said it aloud but I'm sure it occurred to him as it did to me that had we met in the air during the war we would have tried to kill each other.

We went on to talk about our work. He was serving on the Economic Council of the United Nations as a representative of Japan. I thought about the great number of people throughout the world that he was able to help with his work, and me with mine, and it struck me what a great tragedy it would have been if one of us had killed the other.

When I got off that plane I didn't hate the Japanese people anymore, and I knew the meaning of forgiveness.

Author's Note: *Kendall W. Anderson related this account of his unexpected meeting with his old enemy to the author in September of 1990. Ken served as a pilot with the 39th Fighter Squadron in the Southwest Pacific in World War II. He is a graduate of Bangor Theological seminary and served pastorates in New England and Wisconsin before retiring in 1984. Ken resides in Turtle Lake, Wisconsin, where he does some counseling and serves as the editor of the 39th Fighter Squadron Association Newsletter.*

A Source Of Comfort

. . . I will turn their mourning into joy, I will comfort them and give them gladness for sorrow.
                                        Jeremiah 31:13b

When Curt was sent to Viet Nam in 1968 I remember feeling fear in a way that I had never experienced it before. It was different from the fear I had known as a fighter pilot in World War II. I had been shot at, seen friends shot down and killed, been frightened almost out of my wits more times than I cared to remember, but this was far worse. I felt a deep, abiding, terrible dread. Curt was my oldest son. I didn't want to let him go.

I ran into my friend, John Oliver Nelson, up at Kirkridge one day several months after we received word of Curt's death. He asked me to tell him about it. I told him that when I looked out the window that day and saw the Major coming up the walk, I knew why he had come before I opened the door. He told us Curt's helicopter had been shot down, that it had crashed and burned, and Curt was missing. Two days later he came back to tell us Curt's body had been found. As soon as he said, "Your son is dead," I realized I had suffered a terrible loss, but I knew too that my wife and I were not alone in that loss. Someone else's son was a killer and his parents had to live with that. So we all had reasons for grieving.

He listened to me for a long time. John had a mature kind of compassion. His listening, indeed his very presence, was comforting and healing. I shared feelings and thoughts with him that I had not been able to say out loud to anyone else. When I had said all I needed to say, John said to me, "Ken, I would like you to consider going to Viet Nam as the head of the Aid Mission." Because of the malaria and other diseases

29

I contracted in the South Pacific during the war I knew that I couldn't go. I would have been a detriment to the mission. But just the offer in the midst of that kind of grief and depression was greatly comforting. I value it even now.

Author's Note: *Curtis Stewart Anderson, born June 10, 1947, was killed in action January 17, 1969, in Viet Nam. His body is buried at Fort Snelling Military Cemetery in Minneapolis. Kendall W. Anderson related this account to the author in September of 1990. Ken resides in Turtle Lake, Wisconsin.*

I Have Seen God

*Arise, shine; for your light has come, and the glory
of the Lord has risen upon you . . . . Then you shall
see and be radiant; your heart shall thrill and rejoice
. . .*

Isaiah 60:1, 5a

It had been an unusual Sunday school class, the most unusual class Kathleen could remember, and she was troubled
as she reflected on what she had said and done. It had all started
with a discussion about God. One of the children had asked
what God looked like. Kathleen had begun to tell her that no
one has ever seen God, and that God is spirit, when Billy Winston broke in saying, "I have seen God. I can tell you exactly
what God looks like."

Kathleen had responded sharply and quickly. "This is no
time for telling stories, Billy Winston. You shouldn't say such
things."

Billy had been quiet after that, and a pall fell over the whole
group. There was no more discussion about what God looked
like. Kathleen felt immediately that she had said the wrong
thing. But try as she might she could not undo what had been
done. The class ended on a sour note. It bothered her so much
that she couldn't concentrate at all during worship and when
people spoke to her after the service, she responded as if in
a daze. She wondered what she could do to make amends to
Billy and the rest of the class.

Kathleen saw Billy and his parents standing by the water
fountain and went over to talk to them. She began by apologiz-
ing to Billy. "I had no right to say what I did when you said

31

you had seen God. It was very insensitive of me, and I want you to know how sorry I am.

"It's okay," Billy told her.

"Now," Kathleen said, "if it is all right with your parents I would like to hear you tell about how you saw God."

Billy looked at his mom and dad, and they nodded for him to go ahead.

"It happened last year when I was very sick," Billy began. "I thought I was going to die, and I think I almost did. It was all kind of strange, almost like a dream, but I know it was real. I was climbing up a stairway into a long, deep tunnel. When I looked down I saw Mom and Dad and the nurse standing over me by the bed. When I looked up I saw a bright light at the end of the tunnel. I was pulled toward the light, and felt myself floating around it. It was the most beautiful thing I have ever seen. It made me feel warm and safe all over, like when we cuddle at night before I go to bed. Then I heard a voice telling me it was time to go back, that Mom and Dad needed me. I didn't want to leave, but God said (I know it was God) that I had a long life to live and that I would never be alone. So here I am. I felt a lot better after that. Do you remember, Mom? That's when I woke up and you told me how glad you were that I was back."

"Yes," Billy's mom said, "I remember. You had been unconscious for several hours, and we had been afraid that you were going to die."

"But why didn't you tell us what happened?" Billy's dad asked.

"I don't know," Billy said. "I guess I didn't think anyone would believe me."

"I believe you," Kathleen said. "And I'm glad you told us about it. How wonderful it must have been to be so close to God. If you are willing, and your Mom and Dad agree, I would like to have you tell all the children and their parents about it next Sunday."

Everyone agreed, and that afternoon Kathleen got on the phone and invited all the children and their parents to a most unusual Sunday school class.

Author's Note: *This is a fictional account of a child's near-death experience. For more information about such real life experiences, read "Closer To The Light" by Dr. Melvin Morse and Paul Perry, (Villard Books, Random House Inc., 201 E. 50th Street, New York, NY 10016, 1990).*

With You I Am Well Pleased

. . . and the Holy Spirit descended on him in bodily form like a dove. And a voice came from heaven, "You are my Son, the Beloved; with you I am well pleased."

Luke 3:22

Steve couldn't believe what he had just done. He had gotten up in the middle of the sermon and walked out of the sanctuary — and he didn't know why. He felt angry inside, so angry that he couldn't sit still for one minute longer, but he didn't know what his anger was about. Was it something the pastor said? He wasn't sure. Steve tried to remember what the pastor had been talking about but he couldn't remember anything about the sermon. He felt embarrassment for himself and for his family. It wouldn't have been so bad if they had been sitting in the back, but they had been up front in the third pew, their usual spot since the kids had been old enough to sit with them through worship. How would he explain it to them? Should he say that he had felt sick? Steve decided to walk home to spare everyone the awkwardness of explanations after the service. He would tell them exactly what had happened and apologize for his abrupt exit when everyone got home.

Later that afternoon after a long talk with his wife in which neither of them had been able to come to any understanding about the source of his anger, Steve decided that he needed to talk to someone outside the family. He phoned the pastor, apologized for disturbing him on a Sunday afternoon, and asked if he could see him some time in the next few days. The pastor suggested that they meet on Tuesday evening. "That will be fine," Steve told him. He felt some relief just knowing he had taken some action that might help to sort things out.

"Are you still feeling angry?" the pastor asked Steve after he told him why he had left the service early on Sunday.

"Yes," Steve said, "And I still don't know why. It doesn't make any sense to me."

"Tell me everything you remember about Sunday morning, starting with whom you talked to when you arrived at church and everything you can remember about the worship service," the pastor suggested.

Steve told about whom he had talked to and, as best he could, recalled what had been said. He remembered nothing that seemed significant, certainly nothing that was in any way upsetting. Then he described what he could remember about the worship service. The pastor was surprised at how much he remembered. He ticked off every act of worship, precisely in order, naming each hymn and summarizing the content of the prayers and the first two Scripture readings as if he had the bulletin before him. But when he came to the reading of the gospel he couldn't remember which lesson had been read or what it was about.

"It is interesting that you remember the Old Testament and epistle readings but you don't remember the gospel." The pastor reached up and took a Bible down from the shelf. "Perhaps it might help to hear the gospel reading again." He began to read.

Steve listened, and as he heard the familiar words about John the Baptist and the baptism of Jesus, he became aware that he did remember hearing them on Sunday morning, but it wasn't until the pastor came to the final words of the text that he knew what his anger was about.

And a voice came from heaven, "You are my Son, the Beloved; with you I am well pleased."

"That's what I always wanted to hear from my father," Steve said, "and now it's too late." Tears came to his eyes as he allowed himself to feel for the first time the deep hurt that he had been carrying for so long. When he was able to go on, he said, "I thought about this when Dad died last year, but I decided that since there was nothing I could do about it, I just wouldn't think about it anymore."

"Perhaps there is something you can do about it," the pastor said. "Let's pretend that your dad is sitting right here in this chair." He pulled an empty chair over and placed it in front of Steve. "Tell him how you feel. Don't leave anything out."

Steve began hesitantly, but after a few moments he spoke passionately, pouring out everything he had been holding back in the depths of his heart. When he was finished the pastor looked at him and said, "What do you think your father would say to all of that?"

"I can't be absolutely sure," Steve said, "but I think he would tell me that everything is going to be all right. That's what he used to tell me when I was a little boy. And then he would pick me up, give me one of his big bear hugs and say, 'That's my boy.' "

When Steve left the pastor's office he felt like a heavy weight had been lifted from his whole being. For the first time since his father died he felt at peace.

Uncle Hilbert

. . . the decrees of the Lord are sure, making wise the simple.

Psalm 19:7b

But God has so arranged the body, giving the greater honor to the inferior member, that there may be no dissension within the body, but the members may have the same care for one another.

1 Corinthians 12:24b-25

Uncle Hilbert used to stand at the front door of the church every Sunday morning and greet everyone as they came into worship. He always had a big smile on his face as he called all of us by name, and he had a special handshake for us kids. It was a rare day when he wasn't there, and when he was absent church wasn't the same. You had the feeling that something essential was missing.

I don't know why we called him uncle. He was nobody's uncle as far as I know. He had a couple of married sisters who lived in the city, but neither of them had any kids. The little kids called him Hilly, but to everyone else he was Uncle Hilbert or just plain Uncle. "Good morning, Uncle," Mr. Tolbert would say when Hilbert stopped in at the grocery store each morning after walking with us kids to school. He had regular rounds that he made every day. He would meet us at the corner at 7:30 a.m., walk with us as far as the playground; then he would stop at the store, visit with Mr. Tolbert for a while, buy some candy or a pop; then he would head over to the feed mill to watch them grind corn and oats. Sometimes one of the men would let him ride along on the truck while he made a delivery to one of the farms outside of town. Just before noon, about the time the curd was beginning to set, you would find Hilbert over at the cheese factory. They always gave him a white hat and let him watch as they cut up the curd. When they were done, Mr. Sweeney would give him a bag full to take home to his mother so they could have fresh curd for lunch.

In the afternoons Hilbert would get out his bike. For some reason his mother wouldn't let him ride it in the mornings. It was a beautiful red and white Schwinn with headlights, reflectors, rear view mirror, side baskets, an oompah horn, a license plate that said Packer Backer, and long bushy squirrel tails dangling from each handlebar. It was the envy of every kid in town. Hilbert used to let us ride it sometimes on the way home from school, until his mother found out, and then that was the end of that.

Hilbert claimed to be more than 50 years old. None of us kids believed he could possibly be that old until one Saturday morning, when his mother was gone, he invited some of us up to his room in the second story of their house and let us watch while he shaved. He also showed us his collections of old comic books and baseball cards. He had hundreds and hundreds of them, many of them over 20 years old. We decided that maybe he was as old as he said he was. I think it was around that time that I asked my dad why Hilbert had never grown up and he said something about some people being born that way.

That was also about the time that we got a new preacher, the one my folks never liked. His sermons were way too long and from the tone of them you would have thought we were the most wicked congregation God had anywhere in the world. The new preacher didn't want Hilbert to stand by the door and greet people on Sunday mornings. He always sent him on some kind of errand about the time people started to arrive, just to get him out of othe way. This was the same preacher who refused to let Hilbert take communion. He said he didn't understand what it meant and it would be a sacrilege for any one to approach the altar under those circumstances. It must have been a long three years for Hilbert, until that preacher finally left and we got one who wasn't quite so particular.

It was about a year after that when Hilbert's mother died and he came to live with us on the farm. We put him up in the spare room, where the hired man stayed when we had one. We kids thought it was great fun to have him around all of the time. He went berry picking with us, and fishing and swimming in the creek. He also liked to help us with our chores, and we were glad to let him. We had to watch him though. One time he hopped on the tractor, started it up, put it in gear, and was headed straight for the barn before Dad saw him and somehow managed to climb on from the back and get it stopped before it crashed into the barn. I'll never forget how mad he was. He yelled at Hilbert for quite a while, and when he was done with him he yelled at us for allowing it to happen. That was the last straw. Dad said it was too dangerous for Hilbert to stay on the farm. He said he was going to make arrangements for him to live somewhere else.

They had a big community meeting at the church on a Thursday night to decide what to do with Uncle Hilbert. Hilbert was there, too. He sat in the back pew with us kids. He didn't greet people at the door when they came in that night, and he didn't smile much, either, as he usually did. We could tell that he was upset. He just sat in the pew and pretended to read one of his comic books.

The general consensus was that Hilbert should be sent to the county farm. Since he had little money, no relatives and no friends who were willing to take him in, it seemed the only logical thing to do. Someone said that Hilbert would be happy there once he got used to it, said they had crafts that he could do and there was bingo on Fridays. Surely he would enjoy that. Why, he would probably be a lot better off there than he could ever be in town where there was nothing for someone like him to do.

It seemed to be all settled when Mrs. Drury stood up and said in a loud, emphatic voice, ''I will not let you send

Hilbert away!'' Mrs. Drury was the widow of the blacksmith, a quiet little woman who rarely said anything to anyone. She was the last person anyone would have expected to speak out at a public meeting. The church became very quiet. Everyone waited to hear what she was going to say.

"When I was sick last year," she went on to say, "Hilbert came to see me every day. He fed the dog for me and watered my plants. I don't know what I would have done if he hadn't been there. I'm not faulting the rest of you. I'm sure you would have come if I had asked you. The point is, Hilbert was there. No siree, I won't stand by and allow you to put him away. He will come and live with me."

Hilbert lived with Mrs. Drury until he died, about 10 years later. It all seems like such a long time ago now. But I still see Uncle Hilbert's smiling face when I walk in the door of the church on Sunday mornings, and in the quiet time before the service, as I prepare myself for worship, I thank God for all that he gave us.

Author's Note: *In loving memory of my uncle, Max Long, my aunt, Mary Long, and our neighbor, Donald Moore. They are the Uncle Hilberts for whose lives I still give thanks.*

Love Never Ends

Love is patient; love is kind; love is not envious or boastful or arrogant or rude. It does not insist on its own way; it is not irritable or resentful; it does not rejoice in wrong doing, but rejoices in the truth. It bears all things, hopes all things, endures all things. Love never ends . . .

1 Corinthians 13:4-8a

The boy didn't know what to do. Dad was drunk again. Mom was at work. How was he going to get to the game? Coach said he was going to start him at forward again tonight. It was his big opportunity to win a permanent spot in the starting line-up. Mom had forbidden him to drive the pickup until he got his driver's license. He would have to take the snowmobile. There was no other way. If he cut across the lake and followed the ditch along the back road into town he would save 20 minutes and almost make it on time. He put on his down leggings and coat, pushed the snowmobile out of the garage, started the engine, jumped onto the seat, edged slowly down the hill in the backyard and then out onto the ice. It appeared to be solid all the way across. He opened up the throttle and felt the power of the machine as it surged beneath him, thrusting him out over the hard level surface. He hunched himself down behind the windshield. The night air was bitter cold on his face but he liked the feel of it. This must be what it feels like to pilot a jet, he thought to himself as his craft began to pick up speed. He didn't see the hole in the ice until it was too late. It was too wide to swerve around and he was going too fast to stop. His last thoughts were of the team gathering for the game — and of his mom coming home alone in the dark. What would she do without him?

When the woman came into the house she found her husband asleep in his usual spot on the couch. There were empty bottles all around, and she could smell the beer on his breath, so she didn't try to wake him. Her son was nowhere to be seen. Where could he be? The game would have been over hours ago. There was a message on the answering machine. It was the coach asking why Jimmy hadn't been at the game. That's when she really began to worry. She went outside to look for him and quickly spotted the snowmobile tracks leading down to the lake. She knew what had happened before she walked out onto the ice, and it was in that terrible, excruciating moment that she made up her mind to do what she knew she should have done years before. She waited to tell him until the day after the funeral. He pleaded with her to stay, as he had always done before and said that he would stop drinking and go into the treatment program. And then he cried, as he always did, and told her he couldn't live without her. But she didn't listen this time. "I can't help you," she said. "I thought I could, but I can't. And now Jimmy is dead because I haven't been strong enough to leave you." Then she picked up the phone and called her brother, and he came with his pickup truck and helped her move her things to the apartment she had rented in town.

The man drank three beers after his wife left and then walked out onto the ice to the hole where his son had died. He fully intended to end his life there, too, but he couldn't bring himself to do it. Something inside of him said no. He walked back to the house, got into the pickup and drove straight to the treatment center in town, climbed up the steps of the front entrance and rang the bell. When they opened the door to let him in, he said, "I don't know if there is any hope for me, but I have nowhere else to go."

Molly's Comfort

Blessed are you who weep now, for you will laugh.
Luke 6:21b

Blessed are those who mourn for they will be comforted.

Matthew 5:4

There was once a little girl named Molly who had a big Black Labrador dog named Flap Jack. She called him Flap Jack because he liked to eat pancakes. Pancakes were his favorite food. Whenever Molly's mother made pancakes for breakfast, she made about a dozen for the family and two dozen for Flap Jack!

It many ways Flap Jack was like a best friend. He and Molly did everything together. Flap Jack would meet her at the door every day after school, and then off they would go. Sometimes they went exploring in the woods, or fishing down at the pond. Whenever Molly got a nibble, Flap Jack would swim in after the fish. Flap Jack always scared all of the fish away, but Molly wouldn't go without him. At night Flap Jack slept at the foot of Molly's bed. It made her feel safe and warm inside just knowing he was there.

One day when Molly came home from school, Flap Jack wasn't there to meet her. She called, "Here Flappy," at the top of her voice, but he didn't come. She looked everywhere for him, in her bedroom, in the basement, in the woods, and down by the pond, but Flap Jack was nowhere to be found.

That night one of their neighbors came to the door. He said he was very sorry to have to tell them that their big black dog had been run over by a car. At first Molly couldn't believe what she had heard. Flap Jack dead? It just couldn't be!

Molly ran into her room and slammed the door. She sat very still in the darkness for a long time, thinking about all the wonderful times she and Flap Jack had shared. After a while her dad came in and asked how she was doing. Molly didn't say a word. She just climbed up on his lap, put her head on his shoulder and cried until she couldn't cry anymore.

Molly was sad for a long time. In fact she began to wonder if she would ever get over being sad. Life wasn't the same without Flap Jack. Her parents offered to get her another dog, but Molly didn't think another dog would help. There weren't any other dogs like Flap Jack.

One day, after school, Molly stopped to see her old neighbor, Mrs. Wilcox. Mrs. Wilcox was almost 90 and had lived up the road from Molly's house for as long as anyone could remember. She took one look at Molly and said, "You're feeling sad, aren't you? Come in and tell me about it right now." Well, that was all it took. Molly told her the whole story, and when she had finished she said, "And now I'm all alone and I don't know what to do."

Mrs. Wilcox said, "I can't tell you what to do, but I can tell you what I did when I felt like you feel." She said, "When my husband Jack died 15 years ago, I was devastated. I thought I would never get over it. How could I go on living without Jack? We had been married for 50 years. I felt sorry for myself for months and months. I decided to pray about it one day and it was then that it came to me almost as if God was speaking to me directly: 'Look around you. You are not the only one who is sad. Go and help others who are sad. You can do it best because you know how they feel!' So I went," Mrs. Wilcox said. "Whenever I heard that someone had lost a loved one, I made it my business to go to them and let them know that I cared. And do you know, Molly, I discovered that God had given me a special gift. I was able to help other people feel better, and that made me feel better, too."

Molly never forgot what Mrs. Wilcox told her. Whenever she heard that someone had lost a pet, a friend, a grandpa or a grandma, she was there to let them know that she cared.

And do you know what? One day Molly discovered that she wasn't sad anymore. In fact, she was bursting with joy because her caring had helped so many people who had been feeling sad.

The Other Cheek

If anyone strikes you on the cheek, offer the other also; and from any one who takes away your coat do not withhold even your shirt.

Luke 6:39

A little boy was on his way to school one day when three big boys stopped him and began to tease him. They called him names, they made fun of his clothes and they took his lunch. One of the big boys ate his sandwiches, another ate his apple, and the third ate his oatmeal cookies and drank his milk. Then they all ran away laughing and congratulating themselves on the fine prank they had pulled.

The little boy was very upset. He went hungry that day, and he wondered to himself what he would do if they took his lunch every day. That night, when he got home, he told his mom and dad what had happened, and asked them what he should do.

His dad said, "You might do what Jesus suggested. Jesus said. 'If someone hits you on the cheek, offer to let him hit the other one, too, and if someone steals your coat, give her your shirt, too.' "

The little boy thought that sounded very strange, and he asked his dad what he meant. His dad came close and then he whispered something in his ear. The little boy smiled and said, "That's just what I will do."

The next day, on the way to school, the big boys stopped the little boy again. They teased him, they called him names and they made fun of his clothes. But when they started to take his lunch, the little boy said, "Wait, I have something for each of you."

46

The big boys stopped. They didn't know what to think. What could the little boy possibly have for them?

The little boy smiled, reached into his bookbag and took out three lunches. "I brought a lunch for each of you today so you will all have plenty to eat."

The big boys didn't know what to say. One boy said, "No thank you." But the little boy said, "Take it. I want you to have it."

The other kids who were watching began to laugh. The big boys were so ashamed that they dropped their lunches and ran away.

Later that day the little boy found the big boys on the playground and told them how sorry he was that the other kids had laughed at them. He said, "I didn't mean to make you feel bad, I just wanted to stop you from taking my lunch again. I hope you will forgive me. I would like it very much if we could be friends."

Her Shining Face

As he came down from the mountain with the two tablets of the covenant in his hand, Moses did not know that the skin of his face shone because he had been talking with God.

Exodus 34:29b

And while he was praying, the appearance of his face changed, and his clothes became dazzling white.

Luke 9:29

"She was very old. All of her friends are dead. I'm her only family. I think a small, private service is what she would have wanted."

I tried to convince her to have a public service so that her aunt's friends and neighbors would have an opportunity to express their grief and celebrate her life, but she was adamant.

"I don't think Aunt Mae would have wanted all of that fuss."

She was her aunt's only surviving relative. She admitted that they hadn't seen each other for a number of years, but insisted that they had been close when she was a child.

"I used to spend summers with her and Uncle Ralph," she said. "They let me help them wait on tables in the restaurant."

"Then surely you must know about all the friends they had, and how greatly loved they were by everyone in this community." That's what I wanted to say, but I didn't say it. She had made up her mind before she arrived, probably before she got on the plane.

We went on with the funeral plans according to her wishes. She and the funeral director, and I, were the only persons present at the service. I went through the whole ritual, and shared what I knew about Mae's life and witness before I preached the sermon. But it didn't seem to be enough. I felt like I had failed Mae, and I was angry with her niece for being so insensitive. As the funeral director and his hired help carried her coffin out the door of the church, I looked at all of the headstones in the cemetery that also served as our church yard, and thought to myself, "These are your mourners, Mae." And so I prayed with them, the congregation of the dead, as we placed Mae's body in her grave and committed her to God.

I was surprised to see Mae's niece in church the following Sunday morning. She said she had stayed in town to take care of her aunt's estate. And I was more than a little surprised to see that the church was full. Every pew was packed, and the ushers had set up extra chairs in the back. I couldn't imagine what the occasion was. I looked at their faces as I stepped into the pulpit. Over half of the congregation consisted of people I didn't recognize. "Perhaps someone is having a family reunion," I thought to myself. But it seemed odd that no one had mentioned anything to me.

The worship service went along as usual till we came to the time for sharing joys and prayer concerns. I gave the invitation to share and immediately Mabel Leoni stood up and said, "Pastor, would it be all right if I tell a little bit about the life of my friend, Mae Banning?" She was trembling as she spoke. I could tell this was very difficult for her. I said a quick prayer for her under my breath and then out loud said, "Yes, I think that would be most appropriate. Go right ahead."

"Mae was my best friend," she began. "We went to grammar school together and we've been close ever since. But that's not what I want to share. It's her Christian witness that I would like everyone to hear about. As most of you know, she and Ralph operated the Gothard Street Cafe for over 40 years. For those of you who are new in town, it was where the donut shop is now, across from the frat houses and sororities on what we used to call "College Row." The college kids would stop in

49

after their classes for a soda or a shake. Mae and Ralph were like a mom and dad away from home to a lot of those kids. A good many of them would never have made it through school without their support. They helped kids find part-time work, they loaned them money, they even helped them with their course work. Mae used to tutor the kids who were having trouble with their math. She would sit them down in the back booth and make them do their figuring over and over again till they got it right. When a girl or a boy came in with a broken heart over some failed romance, Mae would listen for a while and then when they had cried all of their tears, she would say, 'Now remember, there is more than one fish in the sea.' Sometimes someone would come in who was in serious trouble, an expulsion notice for poor grades, a pregnancy, or maybe they had been caught cheating on an exam. Mae had a way of recognizing trouble when she saw a sad face hanging over a cup of coffee. She would ask Ralph if he could handle things for a while. Then she would ask whoever it was to join her in that back booth. 'Now, tell me what's wrong,' she would say. And before long they would pour it all out. Mae was a good listener, but she did more than that. She would send them to a pastor or a school counselor — and most of her back booth counseling sessions ended in prayer. Ralph used to say that Mae was in her glory when her kids were around. 'Her face just shines,' he said. They brought out the best in her. And they loved her, too. A great many of them kept in touch after graduation. She received letters, Christmas cards, wedding invitations and birth notices from all over the country. And they always came to see her when they were in town. I could go on and on,'' Mabel said, ''but that's enough. Mae did the Lord's work and I just thought it should be said.''

When she sat down there followed a long reverent silence. And then one by one the strangers in the congregation stood up to tell what Mae had meant to them. They were Mae's kids, come back to give thanks for her life. I learned later that they were all there because Mabel had called them.

When the service was over, Mabel led us all out to Mae's grave in the churchyard. We stood around the grave and no one said anything for quite a while. I finally offered a brief committal prayer and then someone started to sing, "Blest Be The Tie That Binds." We all joined in. I looked over at Mae's niece who was standing at the foot of the grave, and was surprised to see that her face was shining and she was singing, too.

A Walk With The Devil

Then the devil led him up and showed him in an in-stant all the kingdoms of the world. And the devil said to him, "To you I will give their glory and all this authority; for it has been given to me, and I give it to anyone I please. If you then will worship me, it will all be yours."

Luke 4:5-7

The devil came to me the other day, as he often does, and he said, "Preacher, how about joining me for a little walk. It never hurts to walk and talk a little bit, now does it?" I had to admit that I couldn't see any harm in walking and talking, and so I agreed to walk with him for a little while. He led me out the door of the church and up the street to one of our neighborhood convenience stores. He took me up to the counter and said, "I'll tell you what, I'll buy you one of these lottery tickets. He took out his wallet, flashed a large wad of bills, paid the cashier and handed me the ticket. My hands were trembling as I took it. I knew the jackpot this week was $40 million. "Hang on to that ticket and you will be a big winner," he said. "You won't have to work another day in your life." I didn't want to be impolite, so I discreetly put the ticket into my pocket as we left the store, thinking to my-self, "I'll tear it up later, after he's gone."

Then he took me up and showed me all the great pulpits of the church in a moment in time. I saw Riverside Church, and the pulpit of the great Harry Emerson Fosdick, and the Crystal Cathedral in all of its splendor. I imagined myself in a beautiful blue robe, preaching to a television audience of millions. "All of this can be yours," he said. "I can build you a cathedral even bigger and grander than this one, and you will have more viewers than any other preacher in history. To you I will give all of this authority and glory, for it is mine to give, and I can give it to whomever I choose. If you help elect me Bishop, it shall all be yours."

I gulped as I looked at all of those influential pulpits in big churches that are coveted by so many preachers but I want you to know that somehow I managed to say, "No, thank you, I'll stay here in my little church where I'm loved and appreciated."

And then the devil took me to the top of the Sears Tower in Chicago. He let me look through the telescope they have up there at a net he had set up on the pavement below. There was a large crowd gathered around the net. They were chanting, "Go go go, go for it." I could see the television crews from CBS, ABC and CNN setting up to film the action. "Go ahead, jump," the devil said. "It's never been done before. Just think, you will be in *The Guinness Book of World Records*. There will be endorsements, talk shows, movie contracts. Think of all the souls you will be able to save when you are famous. Don't worry about the risk. God will keep you safe. Come on, go for it."

I think that was when I fainted. I'm afraid of heights. And when I came to, the devil was gone, at least for the time being. But I have a feeling that I've not seen the last of him.

Come to think of it I still have that lottery ticket here in my pocket. I'll put it over here in front of the altar for safe keeping. If any of you would like to have it, you are welcome to take it and scratch it off.

Author's Note: *I tell this story as part of a sermon on temptation. I buy an actual lottery ticket at a local convenience store, the kind one has to scratch off to win. Then I place it on a stand in front of the altar and use it as a symbol of temptation in our society. I tell the congregation that I was led to purchase it, but not to scratch it off. I give them permission to scratch it off if they wish. In one church where I told the story, people asked me for months afterwards if I ever scratched off that ticket. I never did.*

The White Buffalo People:
A Covenant Trilogy

The Covenant

Then he said to him, "I am the Lord who brought you from Ur of the Chaldeans, to give you this land to possess." But he said, "O Lord God, how am I to know that I shall possess it?" He said to him, "Bring me a heifer three years old, a female goat three years old, a ram three years old, a turtle dove and a young pigeon." He brought him all these and cut them in two, laying each half over against the other; but he did not cut the birds in two.

When the sun had gone down and it was dark, a smoking fire pot and a flaming torch passed between these pieces. On that day the Lord made a covenant with Abram, saying, "To your descendants I give this land, from the river of Egypt to the great river, of the Euphrates . . ."

Genesis 15:7-10, 17-18

Once upon a time, in the long, long ago, when the world was young and people lived in caves deep in the bowels of the earth, there was a nation known as the White Buffalo people. The Buffalo people had a covenant with the great spirit Yah. The symbol of the covenant was the white buffalo, a rare creature, a freak of nature which occurred naturally in the great herds only once every several generations. Because of their symbolic importance, a sacred stock had been bred over the years and kept in sheltered glens near the tribal caves. The white bulls grew to be eight feet high and weighed more than 2,500 pounds. When a great white bull bellowed, the whole forest and the prairie around were filled with his mighty voice. The sound echoed from cavern to cavern, deep in the caves where the tribes made their home. As long as the voice of the great bulls could be heard in the nation, the people felt safe and secure. They knew that Yah was protecting them.

Every seven years, the 12 tribes of the nation would gather at the mother cave to renew their covenant. The mother cave was the place where Yah had made the covenant with the earliest ancestors of the nation, Ebrayah and Clarah. Every person in every tribe could trace his or her roots back to Ebrayah and Clarah. So, when they all came together it was a great reunion.

The celebration began with the lighting of the sacred fire. Every tribe brought a log specially cut from a tree in front of their cave. A priest from each tribe, in turn, threw the log representing his tribe into the fire pit and shouted, "This log represents the tribe of Oolah, praise Yah." "This log represents the tribe of Trelah, praise Yah." "This log represents the tribe of Eelah, praise Yah," until there were 12 logs piled high in the fire pit. Then the high priest brought a torch which had been kept burning in the back of the mother cave for seven years. He walked around the sacred logs three times, holding the torch high above his head, and as he walked he chanted:

> *Fire, fire, breath of Yah,*
> *Burn, burn, reveal your power.*

And then, as he lit the sacred logs, the people breathed "Yah, Yah, Yah," until the flames were leaping high into the sky. When the fire was burning its brightest, they all joined hands and danced around the fire singing,

> *Buffalo, Come and sing your song.*
> *We are here to greet you son of Yah.*
> *Consecrate the covenant*
> *Green grass, blue skies ever*
> *Praise to Yah, Praise to Yah,*
> *Our almighty protector, Yah.*

55

They danced and sang until they fell down exhausted. Then came the highest, holiest moment of the gathering.

Twelve priests, dressed in buffalo robes, came out of the mother cave leading the biggest white buffalo anyone had ever seen. He was well over nine feet tall. There was no doubt that he was the biggest and the fiercest creature in all the land. He followed the priests as if he knew exactly what he had to do. When they came to the center of the circle, the buffalo raised his head and bellowed into the night. The sound was so loud that the earth seemed to tremble beneath his feet. At that very instant the high priest raised his spear and thrust it deep into the buffalo's heart, and the great beast fell down dead. Quickly the priests drew their knives and cut the carcass in two. Gently, and solemnly, they placed the two halves side by side on the sacred fire. Then the high priest picked up a flaming torch and marched in a figure eight around the two halves chanting:

> *Fire, fire, breath of Yah,*
> *Burn, burn, reveal your power.*
> *The grass is green, the sky is blue,*
> *The Buffalo people depend on you.*

When the chant ended, all of the people came forward, one by one, and knelt in front of the fire. The high priest dipped his finger into the white buffalo's blood and then marked each one's forehead with the sign of the covenant, saying:

> *Blood brother, remember the promise.*
> *Blood sister, remember the promise.*

The last one to come was a little boy named Joshua. His eyes filled with wonder and amazement as the high priest marked his forehed with blood and said, "Remember the promise." As the priest turned to leave, Joshua said very quietly, as if talking to Yah alone, "I'll remember."

The White Buffalo People:
A Covenant Trilogy

The Exodus

But Moses said to God, "Who am I that I should go to Pharaoh, and bring the Israelites out of Egypt?" He said, "I will be with you; and this shall be the sign for you that it is I who sent you: when you have brought the people out of Egypt, you shall worship God on this Mountain."

Exodus 3:11-12

The Buffalo people prospered for many years. Yah kept covenant with them, and they kept covenant with Yah. The grass was always green and the sky was always blue.

But gradually, over the years, things began to change. Fewer and fewer of the tribes came to the mother cave during the seventh year to renew the covenant.

Some of the tribes became so greedy for skins and meat that they killed more than their fair share of buffalo. The great beasts became harder and harder to find. The sacred white buffalo were no longer kept separate from the wandering herds, and soon the sign of the covenant was almost gone from the land.

Other tribes began to cut more than their share of timber. They wasted it in roaring fires on nights when no warmth was needed. Sometimes the fires were kept burning for days while people danced and drank the sacred wine until they were drunk.

One day, after a long night of dancing and drinking, everyone in the Oolah tribe fell into a drunken sleep. No one was awake to tend the fire. Sparks landed in the dry leaves on the forest floor, near the mouth of the cave. The leaves burst into flame, and in a matter of minutes the whole forest and the prairie around were ablaze. Animals ran in every direction, seeking shelter in the streams or under low hanging rocks along the cliffs. Many were unable to find shelter and succumbed painfully to the smoke and flames.

The people, those who were aroused in time, found shelter in the back of the caves. The fire raged for 40 days and 40 nights, until there was not a tree or bush left standing.

When the people emerged from the caves, they saw around them a smoking sea of blackness. There was not a blade of green grass to be seen anywhere for miles. Smoke and ash filled the air. No blue could be seen in the sky. The sun was barely visible above the smoldering embers of the once lush, green land.

The White Buffalo Nation was devastated. No one seemed to know what to do. Somehow the survivors of the 12 tribes found their way to the mother cave. There they stood in defeated silence, waiting for some sign from Yah.

Finally, after many hours, a young woman named Mirah stood up to speak. There was a gasp of surprise from the people. Women, as a rule, did not speak at tribal meetings. Nevertheless, Mirah spoke and the people listened.

She began by reciting the words of the ancient creed in a mournful voice.

Fire, fire, breath of Yah,
Burn, burn, reveal your power.
The grass is green, the sky is blue,
The Buffalo people depend on you.

"This," she said, "is what we have forgotten. We broke the covenant with Yah, and by breaking the covenant we destroyed everything Yah had given us. Is the grass green? Is the sky blue? Is the bellowing of the White Buffalo heard in the land? No! Because we broke the covenant with Yah."

Then she paused for a long time, and looked searchingly into the smoke-clouded sky. When her eyes returned to the people she said, "We must pray for a new covenant." And she implored each of them to fall on their knees, in the ashes, and pray with her.

All of the people fell on their knees. Some of them fell face down, their bodies prostrate in a gesture of humility and dependence.

After many hours of praying, Mirah got up again to speak. She said, "We will find a new home. Yah will lead us to a new land of green grass and blue skies." And with that she turned and began walking through the soot and the ash. One by one each member of the nation got up and followed behind her. As they walked a voice was heard singing in the back of the procession. It was Joshua, and he was singing the words of the sacred fire song:

> *Buffalo, Come and sing your song.*
> *We are here to greet you son of Yah.*
> *Consecrate the covenant*
> *Green grass, blue skies ever.*
> *Praise to Yah, Praise to Yah*
> *Our almighty protector, Yah.*

One by one the people joined in the song.

It took several weeks to reach the edge of the forest. Then they came to a great desert where they wandered for years and years. The desert seemed to have no end. There was nothing but sand as far as the eye could see. The people had no water and no food, except the little they had been able to bring with them on the journey. As the food dwindled, and the water supply began to run low, the people grumbled among themselves. "It would have been better to have stayed in the burned-out land — at least we had water and a little food." Some of the people wanted to turn back. They sent a group to talk to Mirah, but Mirah refused to listen to their complaining. Instead she asked them, "Who is the Great Spirit?" "Yah," they replied. "Who has taken care of you all of your lives?" "Yah has taken care of us," they said. "You are right," said Mirah, "and Yah will provide for us now."

Just then there was heard a great rushing of wings. Suddenly the camp was filled by a flock of birds. The people killed and roasted the birds and ate until they were full. But still there was no water, and again the people complained to Mirah. Mirah didn't say anything. She just took a stick and began digging in the sand. She dug down about three feet and as she dug water began to ooze up out of the sand, until finally there was a spring of water as big as a buffalo skull gushing up from the ground. All of the people drank their fill and they filled their water skins till they were ready to burst.

Again the people set out. They wandered through the desert for 40 more months. There were many hardships and a number of people died along the way. Mirah was one of them. But at last they came to the edge of a lush, green prairie bordered by a great forest. It was even more beautiful than their own land had been before the fire. No one had ever seen greener grass or bluer skies.

It was Joshua who led them now as they marched into the new land. He stopped when he came to the mouth of a great cave. Then he turned, raised his arm for silence and knelt down to give thanks to Yah. All of the people knelt with him and prayed, "Thanks be to Yah."

The White Buffalo People:
A Covenant Trilogy

The New Covenant

From now on, therefore, we regard no one from a human point of view; even though we once knew Christ from a human point of view, we know him no longer in that way. So if any one is in Christ, there is a new creation: everything old has passed away; see everything has become new! All this is from God, who has reconciled us to himself through Christ, and has given us the ministry of reconciliation; that is, in Christ God was reconciling the world to himself, not counting their trespasses against them, and entrusting the message of reconciliation to us. So we are ambassadors for Christ, since God is making his appeal through us; we entreat you on behalf of Christ, be reconciled to God. For our sake he made him to be sin who knew no sin, so that in him we might become the righteousness of God.
2 Corinthians 5:16-21

Joshua took a stick and dug a fire pit. When he was finished, he stood at the edge of the pit and spoke to the people in a solemn voice.

"Go with your tribes into the forest and find caves to live in and food to eat. In seven years we will return to this place and renew the covenant with Yah. Each tribe will bring a sacred log for the fire. The tribe of Bullah will have the special responsibility of finding a white buffalo for the covenant ceremony."

And so the tribes went out into the forest, found caves, food, water and game like they never had before, but there were no buffalo. The tribes of Bullah looked far and wide, but there were none to be found. No one heard so much as the gentle lowing of a buffalo calf in the entire land.

Seven years passed, and Joshua waited by the sacred fir pit for the Nation to gather. No one came. Not one person came to renew the covenant.

And so Joshua went out into the forest to speak to the people. He found that they had returned to their old ways. They were burning more timber than they needed and they were dancing and drinking around their fires with no thought for the morrow.

When Joshua asked them why they had not come to renew the covenant, they replied, "There are no buffalo. How can we renew the covenant without a White Buffalo? The tribe of Bullah looked everywhere and could not find even a brown one. Surely Yah has deserted us."

Joshua was greatly troubled by what the people said. So he picked 12 faithful people, one from each tribe, and went into the desert to pray. They lived in the desert at the edge of the prairie, for three years. While they were there Joshua taught them the ways of Yah.

On the last night of the third year, just before they were to the forest, Joshua called them all together around the sacred fire. He asked them all to raise their arms to the sky. Then he marched around the fire chanting:

> Fire, fire, breath of Yah,
> Burn, burn, reveal your power.
> The grass is green, the sky is blue,
> The Buffalo people depend on you.

Then Joshua took a knife and cut crossing lines on his wrist, and as the blood trickled down his arm he said, "I am the White Buffalo. Through my blood Yah will give you a new covenant." Then he dipped his fingers into the blood and he touched each faithful follower on the forehead saying, "Blood brother, remember the covenant. Blood sister, remember the covenant."

When the fire had burned down, Joshua turned and began walking toward the forest. One by one the faithful followers turned and walked with him. As they were walking Marlah began to sing the sacred fire song:

Buffalo, Come and sing your song.
We are here to greet you son of Yah.
Consecrate the covenant,
Green grass, blue skies ever.
Praise to Yah, Praise to Yah,
Our almighty protector, Yah.

While Joshua was away in the wilderness, things had begun to change in the forest. The grass turned brown and the sky became overcast and gray. No rain fell, and the people became thirsty and hungry. No one knew what to do. At last an old priest named Eliah came forward to lead. He gathered all of the people together at the sacred fire pit. He built a roaring fire and then he marched around it chanting:

Fire, fire, spirit of Yah,
Burn, burn, reveal your power.

Then he turned and addressed the people in a gruff voice, saying, "I have heard that the one called Joshua, who lives in the wilderness with a ragged band of followers, claims that a new covenant will come through him. He says that he is the White Buffalo."

"No! No!" the people cried. "There are no White Buffalo."

"Joshua," said Eliah, "is the cause of all of our problems. His blasphemy has turned the grass brown and the sky gray."

Just then the voices of Joshua and the faithful followers were heard above the din of the gathering. They were still singing the sacred fire song as they marched toward the people.

When the people saw Joshua, they grabbed him and dragged him to the center of the gathering in front of the sacred fire. He stood there silently while they cursed him and shouted insults.

Then Eliah raised his arms and silenced the people. He turned to Joshua and said, "It has been heard in the land that you claim to be the White Buffalo. Are you the White Buffalo?" At first Joshua didn't say anything, and then, slowly, he began to march around the fire chanting:

Fire, fire, breath of Yah,
Burn, burn, reveal your power.
The grass is green the sky is blue,
The Buffalo people depend on you.

Then he raised his arms and bellowed into the night. His voice was so loud that the earth trembled beneath their feet. It echoed through the forest and over the plain, and reverberated to the farthest room in the back of the cave. Boulders rolled in an avalanche from the top of the cliff over the cave, and rubble filled its mouth.

Just as the sound trailed away, Eliah raised his spear and thrust it deep into Joshua's hart, and he fell down dead. The people picked up his body and tossed it into the fire.

The faithful followers were so frightened that they ran in every direction. Joshua was dead, and they didn't know what to do.

Three days passed and Marlah gathered them together in an abandoned cave on the edge of the forest. While they were eating supper, a huge white buffalo appeared at the mouth of the cave. They were about to run for their lives when the buffalo spoke, saying, "Don't be afraid. I am your friend." It was the voice of Joshua. Marlah ran and embraced him. They all hugged Joshua and rejoiced because he was alive.

Joshua said, "I cannot stay with you. I must go to be with Yah. But I will send someone to guide you. Go now, into all the forest and prairie, and tell my people of the new covenant in my blood. Mark them with my blood and bid them to remember the covenant."

With these words, Joshua turned and disappeared into the prairie at the edge of the forest. Marlah led the faithful followers out of the cave. They went into all the forest and prairie and told people about the new covenant. Wherever they went, people listened and were marked by the sign of the new covenant. The sun came out, the skies turned blue, and green shoots sprang up everywhere among the old brown grasses.

One day, while Marlah was speaking to a large group of people in front of the cave where Joshua had bid them farewell, a sound came from the sky like the rush of a mighty wind, fire appeared and hovered over the heads of each one and they were filled with the breath of Yah. Marlah said it was a sacred spirit, the one Joshua had promised would come to guide them.

Filled with the spirit, Marlah raised her arms and looking out over all the people bid them to join her in singing the words of the sacred fire song:

> *Buffalo, Come and sing your song.*
> *We are here to greet you son of Yah.*
> *Consecrate the covenant*
> *Green grass, blue skies ever*
> *Praise to Yah, Praise to Yah,*
> *our almighty protector, Yah.*

Author's Note: *This is the last of three stories in a Covenant Trilogy. The three can be told as one story on one of these Sundays in Lent, or consecutively on successive Sundays as they are arranged here. I first told these stories around the campfire at Camp Lucerne near Neshkoro, Wisconsin, in the summer of 1983.*

The Sacred Fire Song

Music by Kerri E. Sherwood

Buf- fa- lo, come and sing your song. We are here to

(loco)

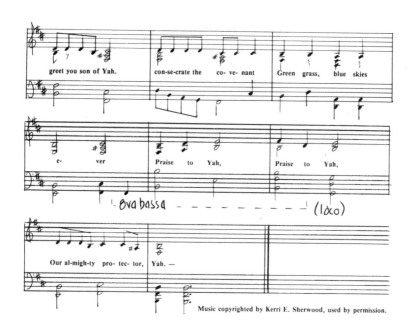

greet you son of Yah.   con-se-crate the   co- ve- nant   Green grass,   blue skies

e-   ver   Praise   to   Yah,   Praise   to   Yah,

8va bassa - - - - - - - - - (loco)

Our al-migh-ty pro- tec- tor, Yah. —

Music copyrighted by Kerri E. Sherwood, used by permission.

The Prodigal Father

Then the father said to him, "Son, you are always with me, and all that is mine is yours. But we had to celebrate and rejoice, because this brother of yours was dead and has come to life; he was lost and has been found."

Luke 15:31-32

There was once a man who had two sons. He loved them both dearly, until he learned that the eldest was gay. "From this day on," he told him, "you are no son of mine. You may stay with us for your mother's sake, but if she dies before me, then you must go." When the mother died a few years later the father was true to his word. He divided her estate between the two sons. To the younger son he gave the family home with the provision that he be allowed to stay there as a member of the family for as long as he lived. To the eldest son he gave all of their liquid assets, about $40 thousand, with the understanding that he was to leave their home and their community immediately. The eldest son protested vehemently, saying, "Dad, I don't want your money. All I want is to remain near you. You are my father, and I will always love you." But the father insisted that he go. "Get away from me," he said, "I never want to lay eyes on you again."

And so, the eldest son took his inheritance and went to live in a distant city where he prospered and made many friends. He was active in the church, and became a leader in the community. He would have been perfectly content except for that place deep in his heart that ached for his father and his brother.

The father lived happily with the younger son in the family home until he married and began a family of his own. The younger son's wife did not like her father-in-law and complained constantly to her husband that he was a burden. When the father had a stroke, they put him in a nursing home, disposed of his personal possessions and moved one of their children into his room. As time passed, their visits to the nursing home became less and less frequent until at last they ceased altogether. The father felt abandoned and utterly alone. The staff was kind to him, and the care was good, but there was no one there who shared his memories, and no one who loved him. He was lonely, and feared that he might die with no loved one near. It was then that he remembered how his eldest son had pleaded to remain close to him, and he thought to himself, "I will call and ask if he will allow me to come and live in a nursing home near him."

When the eldest son heard his father's voice on the phone, he wept for joy and he insisted that he come immediately and live with him and his companion. He prepared a room with a hospital bed, he hired nurses to care for him around the clock, and on the day that he arrived he wrapped his arms around him and kissed him. When the father started to say how sorry he was for all of the wasted years, the eldest son said, "You don't have to say anything. You are my father. I love you. I have always loved you."

When the father died some months later the eldest son phoned his brother to tell him he was bringing their father's body home for burial. He asked if he would help to make the arrangements. The younger son refused, saying, "He was a burden on us all of those years, now it's your turn. After all, he seemed to love you best."

"But you know he always loved you," the eldest son replied. "You must help to bury him, he is your father."

The Friendship Ring

Mary took a pound of costly perfume made of pure nard, anointed Jesus' feet, and wiped them with her hair. The house was filled with the fragrance of the perfume.

John 12:3

It was a bright, sunshiny day and Margie was very happy. It was her birthday. She was seven years old. That afternoon, Margie's mother gave her a party. All of her friends were there. They played games, and ate lots of cake and ice cream. Margie blew out all of the candles on her cake in one blow. Her friends cheered and urged her to open her presents. She got a bracelet, a new blouse, a baby doll, and a book of adventure stories. But her favorite gift was a friendship ring from her best friend, Helen. It was silver and had a red heart in its center. Margie told Helen that it was the best present she had ever received, and she promised she would wear it everywhere.

The next day a beautiful woman came to Margie's school to talk to the students about hungry children. The beautiful woman was a famous movie actress who had given a year of her life to traveling as a goodwill ambassador for UNICEF. (Do you know what UNICEF is?) She told them about all of the hungry children she had visited in refugee camps around the world. (Do you know what a refugee camp is? Who lives in a refugee camp?)

In Cambodia she had met a hungry boy who told her, "Sometimes I cry, but only when it rains, so the other children will not see." Then she said, "You and I can help wipe away his tears."

She told about several refugee camps in Somalia, Ethiopia, Uganda and a little country called Djibouti, all on the

Horn of Africa. "In one of the refugee camps water is so scarce," she said, "that the woman dig in brown mud, and that's what they drink." She told the children that millions of people would soon die in these refugee camps unless the world did something to help them.

In another refugee camp she met a little girl who owned nothing in life but a tiny ring with a red glass stone in it. The little girl had taken off her ring and given it to her to give to some child who needed it more.

When the beautiful woman had finished speaking, all of the students in Margie's school crowded around her to thank her and to ask for her autograph. When it was Margie's turn she stepped up to her and took off the silver ring with the red heart in its center, gave it to the beautiful woman, and said, "When you meet a little girl in one of those refugee camps who needs a ring, please give this to her."

Just then the teacher came up and said, "Oh, no, Margie, you shouldn't give your ring. What would your parents say?" But the beautiful woman said, "Let her give what she can. She may not always have so much to give or the heart to give it."

Author's Note: *This story was inspired by an article about actress Liv Ullman, which appeared in "The Wisconsin State Journal," Section 7, page 2, May 3, 1981.*

A Fist And A Kiss

---

*While he was still speaking, suddenly a crowd came,
and the one called Judas, one of the twelve, was leading them. He approached Jesus to kiss him; but Jesus
said to him, "Judas, is it with a kiss that you are
betraying the Son of Man?" When those who were
around him saw what was coming, they asked,
"Lord, when should we strike with the sword?"
Then one of them struck the slave of the high priest
and cut off his right ear. But Jesus said, "No more
of this!" And he touched his ear and healed him.*
            Luke 22:47-51

Once in Damascus years ago, when I was strolling along
the street called Straight — wondering whether it is truly the
most ancient street in the world that has served continously
as a marketplace — I watched as a man who was riding slowly
through the crowd on a bicycle with a basket of oranges precar-
iously balanced on the handlebars was bumped by a porter
so bent with a heavey burden that he had not seen him. The
burden dropped, the oranges were scattered and a bitter al-
tercation broke out between the two men.

After an angry exchange of shouted insults, as the bicy-
clist moved toward the porter with a clenched fist, a tattered
little man slipped from the crowd, took the raised fist in his
hand and kissed it. A murmur of approval ran through the
watchers, the antagonists relaxed, then the people began picking up the oranges and the little man drifted away. I have
remembered that as a caring act, an act of devotion there on
the street called Straight by a man who might have been a
Syrian Muslim, a Syrian Jew or a Syrian Christian.

Author's Note: *This personal story by Mr. Kenneth W. Morgan, appeared in a letter to the editor in "The New York Times," January 30, 1991, during the third week of the Persian Gulf War. Mr. Morgan concluded the letter with these words: "Now that our American Bicycle has been bumped and soil supplies are being spilled, and angry, unseemingly insults and threats have been exchanged, and war has broken out with the possibility of the loss of myriad lives while millions stand by in horror, when and where can we turn for someone to kiss the American fist, so we can pick up the pieces and go peacefully together along our way?"*

Mr. Morgan also said, in a letter to the author giving permission to print the story in this book: "My reaction to the episode on the street called Straight, some time later, was regret that I wasn't enough of a Christian to have thought of kissing the fist myself."

Mr. Kenneth W. Morgan is professor of religion emeritus at Colgate University. The story was first published on page 172 of his book "Reaching for the Moon, on Asian Religious Paths," ANIMA BOOKS, 1053 Wilson Avenue, Chambersburg, Pennsylvania 17201.

The Nakedness Of Our Fathers

Noah, a man of the soil, was the first to plant a vine-
yard. He drank some of the wine and became drunk,
and he lay uncovered in his tent. And Ham the father
of Caanan, saw the nakedness of his father, and told
his two brothers outside. Then Shem and Japheth
took a garment, laid it on both their shoulders, and
walked backward and covered the nakedness of their
father; their faces were turned away, and they did
not see their father's nakedness.

Genesis 9:20-24

I grew up on a farm in the driftless area; the mountainous, unglaciated part of Southwest Wisconsin where the hills are high and rolling, and the long narrow valleys are accented here and there by towering sandstone bluffs. The farm is bordered on the north by a creek which flows along the bluffs for about a quarter of a mile before it passes under a bridge to the next farm, and on the south by a gravel ridge road which runs off the state highway up about a half-mile to the township dump and then on up past a grove of ironwoods and maples to a wide, level ridge where there are several hundred acres of fields owned by a number of different farmers in the valley below. Tractor traffic is heavy in the summertime as the farmers traverse up and down the road to work the ridgeland. In the evening the road is used as a kind of lover's lane by the older boys and girls of the community. According to local lore, boys will sometimes drive their dates up the road to show them the view from atop the ridge, and then, upon arrival at the end of the farthest field, suggest that they entertain them in a certain way or find themselves without a ride home.

74

Near the bottom of the ridge road, at the bend where the slope steepens and one can hear the tractors backfire as they make their final descent to the highway, there lived a man by the name of Willy Hammenberg, a black man who had moved there from the local shanty town. The shanty town was where the "colored folks," as they were called in those days, lived in shacks and dilapidated houses up against the bluffs, about a mile and a quarter up the state highway and around the corner from the little village which was the center of community life in that part of the county. Gradually, over the years, some of the blacks had married whites and moved into the village. Willy married a white woman and moved south of the village to the ridge road. His wife died tragically, in an auto accident, when their sons were quite small. Willy raised the boys by himself, and supported them on the meager salary he earned working for the canning factory. He was their number one mechanic. Willy kept the pea harvesters running all during the season, sometimes working all night long so that the harvesters would be ready to roll when the crews came in early every morning.

Willy was also known as the town drunk. Was it Mark Twain who said that the town drunk is an elected position? If that is true, then Willy had been elected. His affliction served a peculiar kind of function. His drunken antics were a favorite topic of conversation whenever people paused to visit, at the gas station, after church, and on other such social occasions. "Yeah, Old Willy clipped off another mailbox the other night," someone would say, and then everyone would have a good laugh.

There were always a few days every harvest season when Willy didn't show up for work. The foreman would go and look for him, and when he was found, would sober him up enough to get him back to work. Willy was good at his job. So much so that the company viewed these occasional lapses as a minor inconvenience, so the pattern was repeated over and over again, year after year.

One hot summer day at threshing time, as wagon crews were going up and down the ridge road to collect oat bundles for the threshing machine which was set up on one of the farms below, something happened which the small boy who lived on the farm would long remember. (A wagon crew usually consisted of one man with a tractor and wagon, an older boy to help fork on the bundles, and a small boy to drive the tractor.) It was on the way down the road with the wagon piled high with golden bundles, the man and older boy on the tractor and the small boy riding high atop the bundles, that the incident occurred. As the tractor approached the bend in the road where Willy lived, they saw Willy lying on his back on the ground across the road from his house in the partial shade of a box elder tree. There was a pile of beer cans within tossing distance. Old Willy was drunk again, and by all appearances dead to the world: his eyes closed, his mouth open, and drool running down over his chin. The man and the older boy on the tractor pointed and laughed. They would have a good one to tell when they joined the others down below.

The small boy was troubled. He remembered how kind Willy's sons had been to him during his first year in the small country school which all of the children in the valley around the village attended — all eight grades in one room. He remembered how Willy's sons had helped him with his shoelaces and boots, given him rides when it was too cold to walk, and taken his side when the bigger kids made fun of him because he was the smallest kid in school.

When the tractor pulled into the farmyard he climbed down from the bundles, got on his bicycle, and went back up the road. He helped Willy get to his feet, half carried and half dragged him into the house, put him on the couch, covered him with a blanket, and then left before he could recover enough to see who it was who had helped him.

The answer to the question I am sometimes asked when this story is through is, yes . . . every word . . . except for the last part. I was the small boy who rode on top of the bundles and heard the man and older boy laugh at Willy in his nakedness, and saw him lying there helpless against the assault of their laughter. But I did not go back. Neither I, nor any of the dozens of others who passed Willy on the ridge road that day, all of us good Christian men and boys who went every Sunday to the little white church in the village and sang the hymns of faith and promise, none of us went back. And I wish now that I could.

The Risen Church

This is the day that the Lord has made; let us rejoice and be glad in it.

Psalm 118:24

But in fact Christ has been raised from the dead, the first fruits of those who have died. For since death came through a human being, the resurrection of the dead has also come through a human being; for as all die in Adam, so all will be made alive in Christ.

1 Corinthians 15:20-22

It was a little past 10 on a warm Sunday morning in June. The reporter from the county *Gazette* had stopped with his wife at an old country church. The church appeared to be abandoned, except for a 1969 Ford sedan that was parked off to the side of the lane, under an oak tree, next to the cemetery that surrounded the church. The couple got out of their car and approached the church and the cemetery. She had come to do some tombstone rubbings and to photograph the church. The reporter was along for the ride. Sunday was his day off, his respite from telephones, computer terminals and deadlines.

They wandered leisurely around the cemetery, soaking up the sun and enjoying the summery sights and sounds of the woods around the churchyard. They had stopped to examine an old Civil War-era stone when they were startled by a booming voice that seemed to be coming from inside the church:

This is the day that the Lord has made;
let us rejoice and be glad in it.

There was a brief pause and then the voice broke into song:

O for a thousand tongues to sing my great Redeemer's praise, the glories of my God and King, the triumphs of his grace.

The voice sang on and on and was just beginning the last of several verses as the reporter and his wife entered the church and took a seat in a rickety pew near the back. He was standing behind the pulpit, a white-haired, thin-faced old man. His eyes were fixed on a tattered hymnal which he held up near his nose with both hands, and from which he was singing with all of his might. The aged pew creaked, and then cracked as they sat down. The old man stopped singing in mid-verse, looked out over the top of his hymnal, smiled a warm, welcoming churchy smile, and invited them to turn to hymn number one, verse five. He had caught them off guard. After they reached for the hymnal there was no turning back. They stood up and joined him in the singing of the rest of the hymn. The familiar tune and words took them back to the days of their youth. They remembered sitting in church with their families on warm summer mornings just like this. And so, when the hymn was all sung and they heard the old man intone, "Please be seated," they sat transfixed as he led them through the rest of the service — prayers, Scripture, sermon, offering, closing hymn and benediction. There were moments in the service when they forgot that there were just the three of them alone in an abandoned shell of a church building with cracked windows and water marks on the walls, where rain ran down from holes in the roof. The soaring voice of the preacher lifted them out of themselves as it rose and fell from shout to whisper. It seemed at times that every pew was full as they must have been on Sundays past when the little church was filled with a living congregation.

After the benediction the old preacher came down the aisle and waited by the door, as if he were going to greet a long line of people. He asked their names as he shook their hands.

They could tell he was excited about their being there. He talked to them for a long time, holding them there longer than they wanted to stay. They finally managed to break away, thanked him for the service, and were turning to go to their car when it occurred to the reporter that this would make a marvelous human interest story for the paper. He turned around, told the old preacher that he was a reporter for the County *Gazette*, and asked if he would be willing to tell him something about his work with the church. The preacher said he would be glad to talk with him some time, but not on Sunday. "Sunday is set aside for God," he said, "Could you come back tomorrow?" They agreed upon a time.

The next day, as the reporter approached the old church at the appointed hour, the '69 Ford and the preacher were nowhere to be seen. The reporter waited for over a half an hour, and when he still didn't come, drove into the village down the road from the church to inquire about him. He was told at the gas station that the old preacher had become ill during the night and had been taken by ambulance to the hospital in the city. When he described the strange service he and his wife had attended at the country church the day before, the gas station attendant laughed and said, "Reverend Firby's been doing that for years. Once in a while one or two of the old widows will make it out there for a service, but mostly he just preaches to empty pews."

The reporter drove back to the city and went straight to the hospital.When he asked for Reverend Firby at the front desk, he was told to wait in the lobby. Someone would come out to talk to him. In about 10 minutes a man wearing a clerical collar came in and introduced himself as the hospital chaplain. He told him that Reverend Firby had died early that morning. He said he didn't know much about him but he gave him the number of the funeral home that was handling the arrangements.

The reporter was surprised that there weren't more people at the old preacher's funeral. The big church on the square was nearly empty, except for a few relatives from out of town and the two old widows from the village. Those who were there were glad to tell him about Reverend Firby's life, and about all of the people who had once worshiped in the old country church. When he asked them why Reverend Firby held services there long after people stopped coming, one of the old widows said, "Reverend Firby used to say, 'If no one else is here, God is here, and God hears my prayers for all of God's people.' " "And then," she said, "he would always add, 'I felt I heard God say to stay, so I stayed.' "

The next day the reporter's story about the old preacher who preached to empty pews appeared on the front page of the county *Gazette*. On the back page of the same edition, in the classified column, there was listed this brief notice:

> *Worship services will be held as usual at 10:30 a.m., at Zion Community Church on Sunday. Everyone is welcome.*

Everyone in the village, and on the farms surrounding the old church, saw the story and read the notice on the back page. They liked the story, but what they talked about was the notice. That was news. Who was going to lead the service now that the old preacher was dead? No one seemed to know. The odds at first were on one of the widows, but that didn't seem very likely, and they both denied knowing anything about it.

Come 10:15 the following Sunday morning, the old church building was full. Every spot in every pew was taken. Almost everyone from the village and the countryside for several miles around was there. A couple of carloads of former residents had even come in from the city.

At precisely 10:30 the side door opened, and the reporter stepped up onto the platform and stood behind the pulpit. He opened the Bible to the 118th Psalm and read:

> *This is the day that the Lord has made;*
> *let us rejoice and be glad in it.*

Then he looked out at them over the Bible and said, "Let the church say, 'Amen'!" They all said it. And then he invited them to turn in their hymnals to hymn number one, "O For A Thousand Tongues To Sing." One of the women went to the piano and began to play. It was badly out of tune from years of disuse, but no one seemed to mind. They rose as one and sang at the tops of their voices, and as they sang it seemed to the reporter that he had never felt more alive in all of his life. He smiled to himself and thought about the old preacher who had stood where he now stood, and prayed for this Sunday after Sunday — and then he joined with the congregation in singing the final verse:

> He speaks and listening to his voice,
> new life the dead receive; the mournful,
> broken hearts rejoice, the humble poor believe.

Author's Note: *Charles Wesley's hymn "O For A Thousand Tongues To Sing," appears on page 57 of the 1989 version of "The United Methodist Hymnal." It appeared on page one of the 1964 edition.*

Where You Do Not Wish To Go

*Very truly, I tell you, when you were younger, you
used to fasten your own belt and to go wherever you
wished. But when you grow old, you will stretch out
your hands, and someone else will fasten a belt
around you and take you where you do not wish to
go.*

John 21:18

Wilma Petersen chaired the social concerns committee in
her church. She also headed an action group that lobbied the
state legislature on senior citizen issues; she served on the
regional Commission on Aging and was secretary of a city task
force that was seeking a government grant to build low income
housing. When the doctor told her she needed gallbladder surgery, the first thing she said was, "How long will I be laid
up?" When she was assured it would only be four to six weeks,
she said, "Oh, that won't be so bad, I can write letters and
make phone calls while I'm recovering." The doctor frowned,
but he didn't say anything; he didn't think it would do any
good. Wilma was a determined woman. It would take a lot
more than a doctor's warning and a little thing like gallbladder
surgery to slow her down.

Ten weeks later, Wilma was feeling worse than she had before the operation. She couldn't understand why she wasn't
getting better. The doctor suggested that she come in for tests.
When the results came back, he came immediately into her
room and broke the news to her as gently as he could.

"Wilma, I'm sorry to have to tell you this, but the blood
tests show that you have AIDS."

Wilma couldn't believe her ears. How could a 70-year-old
woman get AIDS? "It was in the blood transfusion you

received during your surgery," he said. Wilma just couldn't believe it. What was she going to do?

It wasn't that she was afraid of dying. Wilma was prepared for death, even a slow, painful death, if that's the way it came. That was the way of the world. She had seen enough of death to know that no one was spared. Her husband had died of lung cancer and she had lost a son to polio. It was the thought of telling her family and friends. What would they think . . . that she had been indiscreet?

She didn't tell anyone at first, but as the disease progressed she decided that people had a right to know. It was an incident with a needle that convinced her to tell. A nurse in the doctor's office had been about to give her an injection one day when the needle slipped and she pricked her own finger. The fact that it occurred before the injection spared the nurse any danger of infection, but Wilma could see that it had been very upsetting to her. The nurse knew she had AIDS. Wilma decided that everyone else who came into contact with her had a right to know, too.

The word spread fast. There were many expressions of caring; phone calls, cards, letters and quiet conversations with neighbors and friends. People were horrified for her and sympathetic at the same time — or so it seemed. She felt no sense of rejection until the following Sunday morning when she went to church. She sat in her usual pew but the people who always sat beside her, or in the pews around her, sat elsewhere. She was beginning to think no one was going to sit near her at all, when Kevin Holmstead, that nice young man from the bank who usually sat near the back, came in and sat beside her on the end of the pew next to the aisle in the same spot her husband Frank had always sat when he was alive. Kevin greeted her pleasantly as if nothing had changed. "Maybe he hasn't heard yet," she thought to herself, but something about his manner told her that he sat beside her because he had heard. That was the beginning of their special friendship. From then on Kevin sat beside her every Sunday that she was able to go to church.

Wilma lived just three years from the time her AIDS was diagnosed — and much of the last few months of her life she was in bed at home or in the hospital, too weak to move around on her own. During that time her family members and several volunteers, organized by Kevin, took care of all of her bodily needs. They bathed and fed her and helped her with her toilet, changing her diapers when there was need. They took turns pushing her around in her wheelchair and carrying her from the bed to the couch and back again. But during the first two-and-a-half years of her illness, before she was bedridden, Wilma was very much the crusader that she had been all of her life. She organized a support group for persons like herself who were living with AIDS. She visited AIDS patients in their homes, in hospitals and hospices. Many of them told how they had been forsaken by family and friends, how they had lost their homes and their jobs, how difficult it was to get the medical treatment they needed, and how insurance companies and the government denied them financial assistance. She wrote to congresspersons and state legislators about the needs of persons with AIDS. She lobbied the city council to pass an ordinance which would prevent landlords and employers from discriminating against persons with AIDS. She spoke to church and civic groups, pleading with them to support the human rights of all persons.

On the day that she died, Wilma asked Kevin if he would help to carry on her work. He promised her that he would, and he thanked her for all that she had done. He said, "It will be easier for me because of you."

On the Sunday following Wilma's funeral, Kevin stood up in church during the time for expressing prayer concerns and said, "You all know how important Wilma's work has been in this community. Will you help me to continue what she has started? There are many persons with AIDS among us who need our love and support. A great many of them are members of the gay and lesbian community, as I am. Will you stand with us in our time of need?"

You Will Receive Power

*So when they had come together, they asked him,
"Lord, is this the time when you will restore the
kingdom to Israel?" He replied, "It is not for you
to know the times or the periods that the Father has
set by his own authority. But you will receive power
when the Holy Spirit has come upon you; and you
will be my witnesses in Jerusalem in all Judea and
Samaria, and to the ends of the earth."*

Acts 1:6-8

The alarm went off at five o'clock, as it always did on Sunday mornings. The preacher rubbed his eyes and sat up on the edge of the bed. The pain was still there. It was the first thing he noticed every morning now. Would he have the strength to do it one last time? There had been many Sundays in the past few years when he wakened feeling weak and feverish, certain there was no way he would be able to lead the service. And each time, as he entered the pulpit he had felt himself filled with a power that was not his own.

Today was to be his last Sunday as a working pastor. His disability leave would start the following day. After 35 years of ministry, and at the age of 58, it all came down to one last sermon — on New Year's Day. He had planned it this way. He looked over at his wife, who was just beginning to stir. They had been married 35 years ago today just before he began his first pastorate. No servant of God could have asked for a better partner. They had shared everything together. Without her caring and her faith he could not have endured these past six years.

The cancer had been diagnosed in 1978 — multiple myeloma. The doctors did not expect him to live more than three months. He had not accepted their prognosis, had been determined to prove them wrong, and as he prayed, had felt assurance that he would be healed for ministry. How thankful he was for these extra years. There had been time to savor life, to share precious moments with his children and grandchildren, and to preach as he had never preached before, with a new sense of urgency. People had noticed the difference. The church, which had been at a low ebb when they arrived, was now full of life and promise. That made it easier to say goodbye.

What would he say to them today? The sermon was written, but he knew that on this day he would not stick to the text. He wanted to leave them with a word they would remember, a word that would endure, and strengthen their faith in the years to come. And then he thought of the birds.

It had happened on the Fourth of July in the same year that his cancer was diagnosed. They were on vacation. He had been wakened by the singing of birds about five o'clock in the morning. When he stepped outside the hotel and looked up into the tree, he saw hundreds of birds and he remembered standing in awe and listening to them sing for over a half hour. What a glorious sound as they sang at the tops of their voices their early morning song. Praise be to God!

The church was full that New Year's Day, and the congregation waited expectantly as the preacher stepped into the pulpit for the last time. He prayed for strength, as he always did, and once again felt himself filled with the power. Christ was there with him.

It was really an Easter sermon that he preached.

"We share responsibility for our own deaths," he told them, "as we share responsibility for our lives. Dying is a part of living. What happens to me when I am near death is my business. Since I have a responsibility for my life under God, I also have a responsibility under God for my death. Our goal in life is not to survive, our goal in life is not just to be healthy, our goal is not just to live a long, long life. Our goal in life is to please God as long as we live, regardless of the number of days — and to live that life in faith that we shall live with him forever and ever and ever.''

And then he told them about the birds.

Author's Note: *This story is shared in loving memory of The Reverend Donald E. Sumwalt. The story of the birds and the excerpt from the sermon are taken from a tape prepared by his son Tom Sumwalt. My special thanks to his wife Hazel for other details in the story and for permission to share it here. It is a slightly fictionalized version of his last Sunday in the pulpit, but true in every way to his life and faith.*

Don served charges in Morresville and Greenfield, Indiana, and Ash Creek-Bear Valley, Webster, Markesan, Juda-Union, Oakly, and Chippewa Falls in The Wisconsin Conference of The United Methodist Church. He was born June 28, 1926 in Texhoma, Texas, and he died July 25, 1985 in Chippewa Falls. His remains are interred at Rose Lawn Cemetery in Madison, Wisconsin.

Uncle Don is my inspiration, my model for life and ministry. He lived what he preached as much as anyone I have ever known.

Praying To Win

I will do whatever you ask in my name, so that the Father may be glorified in the Son. If in my name you ask me for anything, I will do it.

John 14: 13-14

Ithaca High School has been known over the years for its championship wrestling teams. I wrestled on some of those teams in the late 1960s when Steve Waterman was our coach. Steve encouraged us to give our best for the school and the team, but he also made it very clear that church, family and relationships with friends came first. His supportive style of coaching and his caring personality fostered a team spirit that, for many of us, resulted in great individual achievements. We knew that he cared about us more than he cared about winning, and that made all the difference. There were many of us in those years who excelled beyond personal expectations and abilities because of the support and encouragement that we received from Coach Waterman. But, of all the good wrestlers I knew at Ithaca, the best among us was one who never won more than a few matches in his whole high school career.

Rolland Spencer was our heavyweight. At five-foot-four, 162 pounds, he was smaller than most of the wrestlers he went up against. Some of them were over six feet tall and weighed up to 300 pounds. He wrestled some guys who looked absolutely terrifying. They were not only big and strong, they were mean. There were several occasions when we tried to convince Rolland to forfeit rather than risk getting hurt, but he always insisted on wrestling, and he always got pinned. Most of us would have quit after three or four matches like that. But Rolland was not a quitter. He went out, match after match, and

89

gave the best that he had to give. After a while we began to root for him just to get through one match without getting pinned.

I have never been one who believed in praying for myself, or for my team, to win. I always prayed that God would help me to do my best and have always been satisfied with that, whether I won or lost. There was, however, one occasion when I prayed with all my might for our team to win. It happened in New Lisbon, at a late season meet against the Royal Panthers. After 11 bouts we were ahead by four points. There was one match remaining, heavyweight. Rolland was to face one of the biggest and best heavyweights in our part of the state. All he had to do was keep from getting pinned and we would win.

It looked like David against Goliath when Rolland went out to stand across from Royal's big heavyweight. We were all yelling and cheering for Rolland at the tops of our voices, and I don't think I was the only one who was praying like I had never prayed before: "Dear God, don't let him get hurt and keep him from getting pinned."

We thought it was going to be all over in the first period. The big man took Rolland down and tipped him over onto his back in a matter of seconds. Somehow Rolland was able to keep his shoulders off the mat until the buzzer went off ending the first two-minute period. The second and the third periods were the same. Each time Rolland was turned onto his back almost immediately, and each time he strained and pushed and somehow kept his shoulders from touching the mat for the required two seconds. The Royal heavyweight pushed him back and forth across the mat several times, trying almost every pinning combination in the book, but this time Rolland would not be pinned. When the final buzzer sounded, the Royal wrestler's arm was raised in victory, but it was Rolland who was really the victor, and everyone in that gymnasium knew it. We all ran out onto the mat, hoisted Rolland up onto our shoulders and carried him off. No champion ever received or deserved more adulation and praise than Rolland Spencer got that night. We whooped and hollered all the way home. And in the few, quiet moments that came in the midst of our celebrating, I thanked God for keeping Rolland safe and helping him to win.

Author's Note: *Rolland Spencer is a self-employed mechanic in Lone Rock, Wisconsin. Steve Waterman is superintendent of schools in Mediappolis, Iowa. The story appears here with their permission. Ithaca High School still produces some of the best wrestlers in the nation.*

Jerry's Faith

. . . only speak the word and let my servant be healed.

Luke 7:7b

In the Lutheran parochial school I attended as a child I was taught to fear God, and that I risked punishment for sin. When I was 17 years old, my younger sister died of a brain tumor, and I began to question everything that I had been taught. I could not understand how God could allow this. Her death left me confused and angry. I became more of a doubter than a believer. I came to the conslusion that I could only believe in myself. I pushed myself, I worked hard; I became an over-achiever and eventually a workaholic. This program propelled me to financial success, but it was accompanied by personal failure. I learned that the love of money can bring financial gains that are accompanied by personal loss. I became an empty person. I couldn't stand success and began to self-destruct. I lost everything, my friends, those who had pretended to be my friends and my family. It was all like an unbelievable soap opera — and before it was over I learned quite a bit about the judicial system, the Mafia, extortion and revenge. There were times when I feared for my life and for the lives of the members of my family. It was the kind of situation that causes one to think about taking his own life. But I wasn't ready for that option. The love I had for my children gave me courage and made me determined to try again. I wanted to be a believer in something bigger than myself, but it was difficult. It would take a miracle.

I carefully planned a comeback. I wanted to be successful again and not make some of the same mistakes. The task seemed monumental. In the process I met an independent preacher named Andy. He worked for me on a part-time basis and we soon became friends. He wasn't pushy with his religion, so I decided to go to one of his church services on a Wednesday night. It was quite unusual to say the least. Wednesday night was testimony night. The opening song service was quite an experience. The songs had beautiful melodies and were easy to sing. When they sang songs like "He Touched Me" and "O, How I Love Jesus," I noticed that many had tears in their eyes as they sang with great feeling. I felt touched by this, and quite uncomfortable. The testimonies that followed were as impressive to me as the song service. People spoke about what God had done for them, how God answered prayer and healed them.

Was this real? Do they know a different God than I do, I wondered? It was all confusing. I didn't know if I could believe it, but I went back to observe more. I knew these people had something I didn't have. I guess it was a simple faith in God. It seemed like a good way to live, but I still wondered if it was real. If there was no God, I think we would have to invent one to keep our sanity. I tried to keep an open mind on the subject. I found myself reading the Bible because I was hungry for truth.

One Saturday night my mother called to tell me that my grandmother was gravely ill. I needed strength to face this so I went to church the next morning before going to the hospital to see her. That morning Andy spoke of the healing power of Jesus. I cornered him after church and said, "Andy, are you sure he heals today?" He was sure. I marked several of the healing promises in my Bible and then I went to the hospital. As I entered the waiting room, I saw that many of my relatives were there to pay their last visit to Grandma. The pastor of her church was about to get on the elevator after praying with her. I stopped him for a brief talk. I said, "Don't you believe God has the ability to heal people?" He assured me he believed that God does have the power to heal, but he added that we all have a time to die. I knew he was right, but a voice in the back of my mind said, "Prove me and know that I am God."

I followed my cousin and his wife into Grandma's room in the intensive care unit. When I spoke to Grandma she regained consciousness, and her smile told me that she was pleased to see her oldest grandson. I got right to the point. "Grandma, do you want me to pray that God will heal you?" She agreed. The four of us held hands and I prayed for her healing. It was a special moment. The nurses and other members of the hospital staff who were present stood with tears in their eyes. When I finished I had a feeling that Grandma was healed. My cousin's wife knew it, also. Grandma fell into a deep sleep.

When we went out to the waiting room, my relatives were talking about Grandma being ready to pass away. The doctor had told them that she would not live through the day. I said, "Grandma is not going to die today. She is healed." I went home and then back to the church for the Sunday evening service. On Monday morning my mother called to tell me that Grandma had made a complete recovery. I said, "What did the doctor have to say about this recovery?" She answered, "He said it was a miracle."

I believe God knew just what I needed. I had the audacity to take God at his word, and God cared enough not to let me make a fool of myself.

Author's Note: *Gerald Wagner shared this story of his grandmother's healing with a new member class in our church in the Spring of 1990. It is printed here in his own words. Mr. Wagner, an independent semi-truck driver, lives in Kenissha, Wisconsin.*

The Spirit Bird

---

*The one who formerly was persecuting us is now
proclaiming the faith he once tried to destroy.*
                                        Galatians 1:23b

One summer morning in a mission camp where I was serving as a teacher of Galatians to junior high youth, a bird appeared at morning devotions, and lighted on the head of one of the girls. From there the bird hopped to her arm and then onto the arm of another camper and then another. The bird seemed to be looking for someone. We learned later that it was indeed a tame bird, the pet of a camper in an adjoining camp. We were also told that some boys in our camp had thrown sticks at the bird and frightened it so much that it would not come out of the woods.

The following night, at campfire, one of the counselors got up during our sharing time and told this story.

When the bird came among us yesterday morning I was reminded of another camp I attended many summers ago when we were visited by a bird in much the same way. It proved to be a most remarkable bird, and the wonders it worked among us I shall never forget. It was larger than the bird we saw yesterday, about as big as a pigeon — black on top with a snowy white breast — with the most peculiar array of feathers I have ever seen. I have never seen one like it before or since. It came to bring us a blessing at a time when a blessing was very much needed.

Our camp was full of dissension. The campers had little respect for the camp, for their fellow campers, or for the counseling staff. They wrote graffiti on the cabin walls and interrupted the counselors with obnoxious noises and giggling during evening devotions. Campers teased one another and called each other hateful names. The counselors had to break up several fights, including a food fight one day in the dining hall during lunch.

There was one boy who was older and bigger than the rest who was the instigator of much of the disharmony and fighting. His name was Johnny. He would start the teasing and then egg others on until a fight had erupted. He got the food fight going simply by daring one of the other boys to throw spaghetti at a group of girls.

Conditions in the camp reached a low point when Johnny's cabin raided one of the other cabins. They dumped their luggage on the floor and threw their sleeping bags in the lake. The director tried everything she could think of to restore order, but nothing seemed to work. She was ready to call some of the parents and ask them to come and take their campers home. And then the bird appeared — suddenly, as if out of nowhere — on a cold and rainy evening as we were all gathered here around the campfire. It hopped softly and gently among us, flitting from one camper to another, lighting on a head here and an arm there, spreading joy and love as it went. The bird stayed with us for several days. Peace returned to our camp.

One of the counselors, a man in his 70s who had been coming to the camp for many years, told us one night at campfire that it was a spirit bird sent by God to show us how to live peacefully together. Johnny whispered to some of his friends that it wasn't true. He said it was an evil bird, and that if we didn't do something, it would spread disease and sickness throughout the camp. After the campfire Johnny's friends lured the bird into the woods with some bread left from their supper and then pelted it with sticks and stones until it was dead. Johnny watched from behind a tree, and later, when the director asked him what had happened to the bird, he claimed that he had had nothing to do with it.

The next day the old counselor and several of the campers carried the bird's body out to the meadow and laid it gently in a shallow grave beneath the shade of a small pine tree. Then they joined hands and prayed the Lord's Prayer. On the path back to the camp as the little band of faithful mourners sang "We Are One In The Spirit," Johnny and his friends jumped down from a tree from where they had been watching the burial and pelted them with water balloons.

Later that week Johnny plotted with his friends to raid one of the neighboring camps. They planned to soak their sleeping bags with water balloons. When they were about halfway down the path the spirit bird appeared suddenly over their heads, as if out of nowhere. It dove down and landed on Johnny's head with such force that he was knocked to the ground. Then the bird perched on his arm and spoke to him in a human voice. "Johnny, you cannot kill the spirit of God. Whenever I am struck down, I rise up with greater strength and power than before. I want you to go back to the camp and tell everyone that I am alive. Teach them to live by the Spirit."

Johnny went back to the camp and began immediately to tell everyone that the Spirit bird was alive. He became one of the most fervent followers of the Spirit, spreading love, joy and peace wherever he went. I know because I am Johnny. I am the one who caused the other campers to fight with each other and to kill the spirit bird. But since the spirit bird spoke to me, I have been living with the Spirit in my heart. I have not seen the spirit bird since that day on the path, but I see signs of its presence everywhere."

Then the old counselor opened a pouch that he carried on his belt and took out a handful of black and white feathers. He walked around the fire circle and gave a feather to each camper and counselor. We closed our campfire that night by joining hands and singing, "We Are One In The Spirit."

Author's Note: *This story is dedicated to the campers and counselors of the July 1990 Mission Camp at Lake Lucerne near Neshkoro, Wisconsin — with special thanks to our director Karen King and my fellow teachers, Isabel Molina Jefferson and Dick and Pat Myer.*

Neither Pro-life Nor Pro-choice

*As many of you as were baptized into Christ have
clothed yourselves with Christ. There is no longer
Jew or Greek, there is no longer slave or free, there
is no longer male and female; for all of you are one
in Christ Jesus.*

Galatians 3:27-28

*For in Christ Jesus neither circumcision nor uncir-
cumcision counts for anything; the only thing that
counts is faith working through love.*

Galatians 5:6

It is the first Monday in October. A large crowd has
gathered on the steps of the Supreme Court building in the
nation's capital. They have come to express their opinions
about abortion. One side is shouting, "The first human right
is the right to life." The other side replies, "A woman's body
is a woman's business." One side is waving placards with pictures of coat hangers and the words, "Never Again." The other
side is waving placards with pictures of human fetuses and the
words, "Adoption, Not Abortion."

As the day wears on, they direct their shouting more at
each other than toward the court. Their voices become louder
and more shrill. Then, with fists clenched and death in their
eyes, the two sides face off; they move toward each other with
banners waving and placards held high like crusaders of old,
pitched for battle. Before any of them can strike a blow, a
stranger appears suddenly between the advancing lines. He
holds out his arms and shouts, "Peace! Be still!"

Immediately the crowd is quiet. Both groups lay down their
placards. He motions for them to sit down, and they sit on

the steps and wait, looking toward the stranger with hopeful, expectant eyes. He looks first to those who are sitting on his right. "I am told there is one among you who is married to one from the opposing side."

A man stands and says, "I am he. And there is my wife," he says, pointing to a woman who is now standing among the protestors on the stranger's left.

"Come here," the stranger says, motioning for both of them to step forward. The woman and man come and join hands as they stand before the stranger. "Why are you here?" he asks them.

The man speaks first. "I am here because of a story told to me by my father. He was one of the first of the allied soldiers who entered Dachau and saw heaps of human corpses, men, women, small children and babies. It was their eyes that haunted him, he told me, that pleaded with him in his dreams, that caused him to declare with every waking breath: 'Never, never again!' When I think of this holocaust of abortions that is occurring in our nations, I see the eyes of thousands of unborn children who will never see the light of day and I must cry out, 'Stop the killing now'!"

Then the woman speaks. "I am here because of the way my mother died. I am the youngest of 12 children. Our mother died when I was one year old. She became pregnant again soon after I was born. The doctor told her that if she had another child, she would die giving birth but that there was nothing he could do to help. There was a law against abortion. So mothers made arrangements to go to an illegal abortionist. She waited on a street corner. A car came by, she got in, they blindfolded her and drove her several blocks to the house where abortions were done. When it was finished she was left alone, in a back room. She bled to death during the night. Thousands and thousands of women died the way my mother died before abortions were made legal in this country. We can never go back to the way it was. I am here to speak for her — never, never again!"

When she finished the stranger looks at the two of them and says, "How is it that you are able to remain married?"

They look at each other, smile, and speaking together, say, "We love each other."

"You are a light in the darkness," the stranger says. "As long as you love each other, there is hope for the world." Then he raises his eyes and looks out on the crowd. "I bid each one of you to make friends with someone who believes differently about abortion. And when you have found each other, go together into the world and bring me all of the children who have no one to love or care for them, and all of the women and men who have suffered because of miscarriages or abortions and still weep for what they have lost."

The people go off into the world, two by two, pro-life and pro-choice together, to seek the ones they have been told to find. And they soon return with thousands of women and men who are still grieving for what they have lost, and thousands of children who have no one to love or care for them.

The stranger raises his arms high over the crowd, and smiles as he blesses them. "Go to each other. Love and care for one another."

The women and men move toward the children and the children run to meet them. The children jump into their waiting arms and the men and women hug them to their breasts.

For Freedom

For freedom Christ has set us free. Stand firm, there-
fore, and do not submit again to a yoke of slavery.
Galatians 5:1

It is the Fourth of July. An old veteran puts on his medals
and makes his way to the park where Independence Day
celebrations have already begun. He is greeted by the inviting
aroma of hamburgers and bratwurst cooking on portable grills,
and the sounds of happy voices floating out over the grass on
a warm summer breeze. The park is full of picnickers gathered
around tables and sitting on blankets under the trees. Children are playing on the swings and slides, and chasing each
other around the merry-go-round. There is a softball game on
the diamond in the far corner, and splashing can be heard as
swimmers cavort in the waves along the beach. A band begins
to play patriotic songs from a stage which has been set up next
to a statue in the center of the park. Later there will be
fireworks.

The old veteran smiles as he takes it all in, and then he
carefully maneuvers himself into a spot where he will have a
good view of all the activities. He takes out a sandwich and
a small thermos of coffee. Then he settles back into his chair
to watch and enjoy.

After a while a group of young people comes by. They select
a spot under a maple tree, not far from the old veteran, and
spread an American flag on the ground. He knows immediately that they intend to use it as a picnic blanket. Anger wells
up inside of him. How could they use the flag that way? They
take out food and beverage and pass it around over the flag.
Then they begin to eat and drink and talk and laugh.

The old veteran is not alone in his anger. Others nearby have noticed the young people and their flag. Murmurs of disapproval are heard all around. Soon a group of irate picnickers comes over to confront the young people. One man yells out, "I fought for that flag! I will not see it abused like that!"

"Hey man, it's the Fourth of July. We're just showing the colors."

"Not like that, you're not. The flag is not supposed to touch the ground."

The sound of their impassioned voices can be heard all through the park. People come from every direction to see what the fuss is about. Before long there is a large crowd gathered around the flag. The shouting continues, with both sides getting louder and louder. Someone goes to call the police.

The old veteran can stand it no longer. He rolls his wheelchair in the direction of the angry crowd. There are so many people now that those on the outskirts cannot see the flag. Latecomers are not sure what the argument is about. The old veteran pushes his way into the center and shouts, "Enough!"

The crowd becomes quiet, more from the unexpected sight of an old man in a wheelchair than the sound of his booming voice. Their eyes go immediately to the stumps that stick out over the seat just above the place where his knees used to be. And then they see the medals pinned to his jacket — the purple heart and silver star. They watch in awe as he raises himself up out of his seat with arm muscles hardened by years of pushing and pulling the wheels on the chair which is his home every waking hour of every day. When his head is almost even with the faces of those who are standing over him, his eyes look down at the flag and he says, "This is not what it's about. It's what it stands for. Freedom. Freedom to choose. Freedom to be."

Then he lowers himself back into his seat, and as the crowd parts he wheels away back to his original spot.

The picnickers go quietly and quickly back to their families. The young people continue their meal around the flag, and the old veteran watches and waits. Soon it is dusk and

102

the fireworks begin. The dark sky explodes with color as rockets go up, one after another. Then comes their noise, boom, boom, boom. Somewhere out on the lake someone sets off a string of firecrackers. Their ack, ack, ack hits the old veteran's ears like the sound of machine gun fire he remembers from the war almost 50 years ago. For a moment he is back in the battle with shells exploding all around him. He hears the cries of the wounded and sees the faces of the dying. He comes to himself in time to see the grand finale, the colors red, white and blue emblazoned across the sky in the form of a flag. "Yes," he whispers to himself, "for freedom."

Neighbor

*Which of these three, do you think, was a neighbor
to the man who fell into the hands of the robbers?
He said, "The one who showed him mercy." Jesus
said to him, "Go and do likewise."*

Luke 10:36-37

An old woman was passing through the park one day on
the way home from the store, when she was attacked by a
neighborhood gang who beat, raped, robbed her, and departed,
leaving her half dead. She was taken to a hospital, treated,
and lay in a coma, unconscious for several days. A pastor came
to see her each day, stood by her bed, folded his hands and
prayed for her release. The nurses came in regularly to bathe
her and to attend to her IV tubes.

One day the old woman's heart stopped. Nurses and doctors came running from every direction. They thrust large tubes
into her lungs and neck; one of the doctors pounded on her
chest, cracking some ŏf her ribs, then she was shocked three
times with an electrical charge that lifted her body completely
off the bed. Her heart began to beat again. They hooked up
a ventilator to assist her breathing, the IVs were reattached
to her arms, and then she was left alone again in the care of
a heart monitoring machine.

Later that evening, a member of the Hare Krishna sect who
was recovering from an operation across the hall, and who
had witnessed all of this, came into her room and looked on
her with compassion. He wiped her face with a damp cloth
and tenderly massaged her forehead and neck with his fingers.
Then he sat down beside the bed, took hold of one of her

hands, prayed with her, talked to her, and stayed with her throughout the night until they came and took him away.

Author's Note: *For more information about this issue see, "Rules On Reviving The Dying Bring Undue Suffering, Doctors Contend." Page 1 and section B6 of "The New York Times," October 4, 1990.*

Prophet's Eyes

So Naaman came with his horses and chariots, and halted at the entrance of Elisha's house. Elisha sent a messenger to him saying, "Go and wash in the Jordan seven times, and your flesh shall be restored and you shall be clean.

2 Kings 5:9-10

Once there was a woman of great faith who was dying of cancer. Her name was Celia Muldroon. She was known in her little community as a kind of Carrie Nation. Celia had preached against demon rum all of her life. She missed no opportunity to inform the public about the danger of alcohol. She wrote hundreds of letters to the editor of the local newspaper, she organized panel discussions and arranged for expert lecturers to come in from the city. Once she even convinced several of her friends from the Tuesday morning Bible study group to join her in picketing Joe's Town Pump on Main Street. Unbeknownst to Celia and the ladies, Joe simply unlocked the back door and business-went on as usual with only a little inconvenience to the regulars. The ladies grew tired of their picketing after a few days and that was the end of that. But Celia never gave up her one-woman crusade, and was slowed, not at all it seemed, by the onslaught of her illness.

It occurred to Celia, after the doctors had tried both radiation and chemotherapy, and it was apparent that medical science was not going to be able to save her, that the Scriptures revealed many instances of divine healing. "I'm a person of faith," she thought, "why not me?" She decided in that moment that she would find herself a faith healer.

Celia had heard that there was an evangelist in the city who held healing services in his church on Wednesday nights. She had never been to a healing service, but she thought it might be worth a try. So she packed a bag, and without telling anyone of her plan, got into her car and drove the 100 miles to the city. She checked into a motel, found the church, and determined the exact time of the service. When the service began that night Celia was there in the front row. She was surprised to discover that people were not healed dramatically or immediately, as she had imagined. The healer talked quietly with each person who came forward, and then prayed for healing — and not always in the same way. Sometimes he laid his hands on the person's head, sometimes on a shoulder or an arm. Sometimes he simply held a hand and prayed silently. Again and again he reminded those who came that healing comes in God's time, and in God's way, not ours. But what struck Celia most were his eyes. "He had prophet's eyes," she told her friends later, "the kind of eyes that see into the heart. He could look at you once and speak to you as if he had known you all of your life."

When Celia's turn came, the healer took her hand, looked into her eyes, and without waiting to hear her story, addressed her in the same quiet voice she had heard when he spoke to the others.

"You will be surprised at what I'm going to tell you," he said, "but if you know the story of Naaman, you will do what I suggest."

Celia nodded to indicate that she knew it. They had studied 2 Kings in her Bible group.

"Go into a bar," the healer said, "order a shot of whiskey, drink it down, and then say in a voice loud enough for everyone to hear, 'I've come to ask God for a blessing.' "

They were more than a little surprised at Joe's Town Pump, when Celia came in the next day. One of the old regulars down at the end of the bar said, "Look out, there's going to be trouble." Everyone thought she had come for some kind of dramatic confrontation. They half expected her to get up on the bar and preach — or maybe to take out a hatchet and smash all of the bottles on the shelf behind the cash register. They couldn't believe their ears when they heard her order a shot of whiskey — or their eyes when they saw her drink it down in one gulp. And when they heard her speak the words she had been instructed to say, they were dumbfounded.

"What did she say?" someone finally asked.

"She said she's come to ask God for a blessing. Pour her another drink." It was the old regular down at the end of the bar.

Joe ignored him. He looked at the strange, sickly old woman who stood before him with the empty shot glass in her hand, and without thinking he stretched his portly frame out over the bar and kissed her tenderly on the cheek.

Just before she died, about two weeks later, Celia told her friends, "A peace came over me in that moment like I have never known before. I felt warmed through and through as if surrounded and held close by some divine presence."

Joe closed the bar on the day of Celia's funeral and closed it for a good three days later. The regulars protested vehemently, but they soon found places in other bars and Joe started going regularly to worship on Sunday mornings. He married one of the ladies from the Tuesday morning Bible study group, and soon became one of the most loved and respected leaders of the church.

The Red Mules

By faith Abraham obeyed when he was called to set out for a place he was to receive as an inheritance; and he set out not knowing where he was going.
Hebrews 11:8

I began helping Dad in the fields when I was 10 years old. The year was 1927, dust bowl days. We lived on a rented farm in the Texas Panhandle, about five miles south of Texhoma, just over the border from Oklahoma. It was so dry and hot that we had one crop failure after another. We stayed there just seven years before pulling up stakes and moving to Wisconsin. It was in the spring of our last year in Texas that Dad decided I was old enough to help. He started me out with a team of red mules. He figured they knew more about farming than I did, and I guess maybe he was right. Kate and Jewel, we called them. They were full sisters. Dad had raised them and broken them to the harness himself. Kate was a yearling and Jewel was a two-year-old when we moved down from Kansas in '21. Oh, they were a pretty team, a soft sandy red, the color of the Texas sky at sunset. And how they could pull. Some said there wasn't a better team anywhere in the country. At threshing time when the neighbors came in with their teams and wagons, they always made sure that the red mules were one of the teams that helped to haul the grain into town. There weren't many roads in those days, and so when we took a load into town we simply followed the straightest route across the cut fields. The wagons, when loaded with grain, were very heavy and sometimes one of them would get stuck in a sand bog. Then the drivers would have to sit there and wait until the red mules came along and pulled them out.

I worked in the fields all that summer. Boy, it was hot. When we were plowing I had two horses along with the mules. Dad drove six head of horses and mules. He had all of them to harness every morning and unharness every night. We turned them out to pasture at night after they had their grain and water, and we had to round them up again first thing every morning just before sunup. They all knew their stalls, so it usually didn't take more than an hour from start to finish. It was a little over quarter of a mile from the house to the fields. We would push ourselves and the animals all morning, before it got too hot, then about noon we would come back to the house, water the teams, eat dinner, take a nap, and go back out again and work till almost dark. It was a half-mile across the field, one way. By the time we drove the teams over and back they were ready for a rest. We figured if we got in eight rounds in a day we were doing pretty good.

Once in a while Dad would drive the red mules when he went into town. It was comical to see those old girls going down the road, their heads bobbing up and down, and their long, pointed ears flapping against their necks. That was their motion, a kind of natural rhythm that helped to propel them along.

One day when Dad was on his way home from town with the mules, a sand storm blew up suddenly, as they often did in that part of Texas. The dirt and dust were so thick in the air he couldn't even see his hands in front of his face. Dad simply dropped the reins and said, "Take me home girls." They had to go more than five miles, down the main highway, onto a side road and around several bends, but them old mules knew where they were going, and they brought him home.

Author's Note: *My father, A. Leonard Sumwalt, tells this story of his childhood on the farm in Texas. It is printed here with his permission and mostly in his own words.*

The Lost Dog

Which one of you, having a hundred sheep and los-
ing one of them, does not leave the ninety-nine in
the wilderness and go after the one that is lost until
he finds it?

Luke 15:4

There was once an old man who had a little spotted dog. The dog was a mixture of spaniel, collie, terrier and dachshund. He was a street-bred mutt, but the old man loved him because he was all he had. They were constant companions, going everywhere and doing everything together. Every night the dog slept at the foot of the old man's bed.

Then one day the dog disappeared. He was playing in the yard one moment, and the next thing the old man knew he was gone. He searched everywhere for him, looked on every street, around every corner, and talked to every neighbor, but the dog was nowhere to be found. The old man searched all over the town, calling out the dog's name as he went, listening in vain for his familiar bark. The next day was the same and the one after that . . . for weeks the old man searched till finally his neighbors and friends convinced him that there was no use in looking anymore. Surely the dog is dead, they said: hit by a car, no doubt, and crawled off by himself to die.

Still the old man would not give up hope. Every night, before bed, he went out on the porch and called out the dog's name at the top of his voice. This went on for several months. The neighbors were certain that the old man had lost his mind. And then one night, as the old man was calling his name, the little spotted dog came home. The old man never knew where he had been or what caused him to stay away so long, but he was very glad that he had never stopped calling his name.

111

The Crooked Accountant

And his master commended the dishonest manager because he had acted shrewdly; for the children of this age are more shrewd in dealing with their own generation than are the children of light.

Luke 16:8

There was a rich bookie who had an accountant who was accused of mismanaging his business affairs. And the bookie called in the accountant and said, "Hey, man, what's this I hear about you? Turn in the books, you're fired!" The accountant thought, "What shall I do? I won't qualify for unemployment and I am too proud to go on welfare. I know what I'll do, I'll make sure that enough people owe me that I won't have to worry when I start looking for another job." He called in all of the bookie's clients, one by one. "How did you do on your last bet?" he asked the first. "I lost $3,000," the man told him. "Let me check that on the computer," the accountant said. "That's what I thought, there was a mistake in the point spread on that game. You only owe $1,500." The next man was in arrears on several losing bets. "How much do you owe all together?" the accountant asked him. "Ten thousand dollars," came the reply. The accountant smiled at him and said, "Pay me 80 cents on the dollar and the slate is clean." And so it went, until the accountant had enough people in his debt that he could be certain of landing another job. When the rich bookie found out what his former employee had done, he bought him a drink and congratulated him on his shrewdness.

The Rich Woman And The Bag Lady

But Abraham said, "Child, remember that during your lifetime you received your good things, and Lazarus in like manner evil things; but now he is comforted here, and you are in agony."

Luke 16:25

There was a rich woman who lived in the penthouse of a big city apartment building. And in a park across the street there lived a poor bag lady named Clara who wanted nothing more than to pick through the rich's woman's garbage. Clara was crippled, and could walk only with the aid of a shopping cart, in which she kept all of her earthly possessions. Moreover, little children used to taunt her as she went about her daily rounds.

The poor bag lady died and was carried by the angels to heaven to sit at the right hand of Jesus. The rich woman also died, and was buried, and went straight to hell and there in torment she looked up and saw Jesus, afar off, and Clara sitting beside him with her head on his shoulder.

And the rich woman called out, "Dear Jesus, have mercy on me, and send Clara to put an ice cube on my tongue, for I am in anguish in this place." But Jesus said, "Remember, in your lifetime you received your good things, and Clara received evil things, but now she is comforted here, and you are in anguish. And, besides all of this, between us and you there is a great gap, in order that those who would go from here to you may not be able, and no one may cross from there to us."

And the rich woman said, "Then I beg you, dear Jesus, to send Clara to my sisters at the club so that she may warn them, so that they may avoid this place of torment." But

Jesus said, "They have bag ladies aplenty living among them; let them hear them." And the rich woman said, "No, dear Jesus, if someone goes to them from the dead, they will listen." Jesus answered, "I have risen from the dead and I live among them in all of the poor and homeless throughout the world. If they cannot see me, neither will they be convinced if someone else should rise from the dead."

Persistence

And will not God grant justice to his chosen ones who cry out to him day and night? Will he delay long in helping them?

Luke 18:7-8

In a certain city there was a corrupt bureaucrat who neither feared God nor respected people; and there was a welfare mother in the same city who kept coming to him and saying, "Make my landlord fix the furnace and insulate the walls. I can no longer afford to pay the heat bills and my children are freezing." For a while the bureaucrat refused to listen, but the woman kept coming to his office every day with her three children, and each day she would make her plea again. After several weeks of this, he thought to himself, if I don't give this woman what is right, she will pester me to death. An order was issued, the furnace was replaced and insulation was installed in the walls.

The next day the woman was back in the bureaucrat's office with her children. She thanked him for what he had done and then she said, "Now let me tell you about my plumbing problems."

The Church Leader And The Drug Dealer

But, the tax collector, standing far off, would not even look up to heaven but was beating his breast and saying, "God, be merciful to me a sinner!" I tell you this man went home justified rather than the other; for all who exalt themselves will be humbled, but all who humble themselves will be exalted.

Luke 18:13-14

Tell this story to those who trust in their own righteousness and despise others.

Two people, one a church leader and the other a drug dealer, went into the church to pray. The church leader prayed thus with himself. "God, I thank you that I am not like other people, welfare cheats, pornographers, or even like this drug dealer. I go to worship every Sunday, I give a tenth of my salary and my time to the church and I spend two weeks of my vacation every summer building homes for the poor." But the drug dealer, sitting way in the back of the sanctuary would not even look up toward the altar, but wrung his hands and said, "God, forgive me, I am a sinner." I tell you the drug dealer went home justified rather than the church leader; for all who hold themselves up will fall, and those who admit their shortcomings will be lifted up.

Gopher Heaven

Some Sadducees, those who say there is no resur-
rection, came to him and asked him a question,
"Teacher, Moses wrote for us that if a man's brother
died, leaving a wife but no children, the man shall
marry the widow and raise up children for his
brother. Now there were seven brothers; the first
married and died childless; then the second and the
third married her, and so in the same way all seven
died childless. Finally the woman also died. In the
resurrection, therefore, whose wife will the woman
be? For the seven had married her."

Luke 20:27-33

Several years ago, when we lived in Marquette County, in
the little town of Montello, our family bought a new house.
It was our dream house and it had everything we had ever
hoped for, but it didn't have a finished yard. The lawn was
nothing but sand and weeds. So we went into the landscaping
business. We hauled in black dirt. We raked and rolled and
seeded and raked some more. We planted shrubs and put in
flower beds. We watered and hoed and waited for nature to
do the rest. By the end of the second summer we had one of
the nicest yards in the neighborhood.

It was near the beginning of the third summer that all of
the trouble began. Holes started to appear here and there all
around the lawn, and flowers began to sink into the ground
and to disappear mysteriously beneath their beds, as if some
kind of underground vacuum cleaner were sucking them into
the earth. We had gophers! I saw one, one day by a hole over
on the far end of the yard. He was standing up straight and
tall, as gophers do when they smell danger, all six inches of

117

him, stiff as a stick. He looked like a sentry guarding his post. I immediately declared all out war. I let out a yell, grabbed a hoe and took off across the yard prepared to commit bloody murder. The gopher waited until the last possible moment and then just as I raised my hoe to strike the fatal blow, he zipped down the hole and disappeared into the depths below. I beat on the ground and yelled some more, but it was no use. I had been out-maneuvered.

What to do? I needed a plan. It was then that I remembered the great gopher wars of my youth. I grew up on a farm, and one summer, after the planting was done, we were struck by a plague of gophers. When the corn came up, the gophers began to nip it off at the roots. Row after row disappeared overnight. Before long it was apparent that the whole crop was in danger. My brothers and I went on gopher patrol. We filled 10-gallon milk cans with water, loaded them on the back of our old B Farm All tractor, grabbed the binoculars and the .22 rifle, and took off for the field. When we came to a hole we would pour in about half a can of water and then watch. If no gophers appeared we would pour in some more water and wait. We knew they would have to come out or drown. Sooner or later one would pop out of the hole at the other end of the tunnel. When we spotted one we would whistle. They would always stand up and look around to see where the danger was. Then I would line him up in my sights, and pow!

I never did actually hit one. But I almost hit one once, and it scared him so much that he rolled all the way down the hill, tumbled over an embankment, skidded out onto the highway, and was run over by a milk truck. We skinned him out and hung his hide up on the barn as a warning to all of the other gophers. And it must have worked because it wasn't long after that till the gopher population was back to normal.

That gave me an idea about what I could do to get rid of the gophers in our yard. I borrowed a pellet gun from a neighbor and began to plot how I would send those yard-wrecking scoundrels to gopher heaven. I would put a ladder up to the roof of the house, and rigged up a hose so I could flood several of the holes at once, just before I ascended the ladder to my look out post on the roof. Then I would pump my pellet gun full of air and wait. When those flower-thieving varmints popped up out of their holes, gasping for air, I would pick them off one by one. It was a perfect plan. I was a military genius. I had visions of myself up on the roof in jungle fatigues, picking off gophers right and left; the Clint Eastwood of Marquette County. "Go ahead Gopher, make my day." It would have worked too, if fate hadn't intervened.

I was taking a nap on the couch in front of the television one Saturday afternoon when my daughter ran in with the neighbor kids yelling, "Daddy, Daddy, look what we found in the yard!" They had an ice cream pail full of baby gophers! There were nine of them wriggling and squirming around in a little nest of grass and leaves in the bottom of the pail. What was I going to do? I couldn't murder them in front of the kids. So I told the kids to put them back in the hole where they had found them so their mother could take care of them. They reluctantly complied.

That night there was a terrible thunderstorm. My wife Jo began to worry about the baby gophers. She put on her raincoat and got out the umbrella and went out in the pouring rain to check on them. She found half of them outside of their hole, wandering aimlessly, apparently abandoned by their mother (I swear I didn't do it — I had only planned to). They were soaked and shivering in the cold rain and wind. She gathered them up, put them in her pocket, reached down into the hole, found the rest, and brought them all into the house. She made a bed for them out of a shoebox and one of my old shirts. Then she warmed up some milk, got out an eye dropper, and became the first gopher wet nurse in the history of the world. What a sight it was. They clutched their grimy little claws around the tip of the dropper and their little lips smacked and popped as they slurped up the warm milk. It was almost more than I could bear.

Jo got up every two hours that night to check on her "poor babies" as she called them now, and to give them more warm milk. But, alas, it was almost all to no avail. By morning all but one of them were dead, and there wasn't much hope for him. We buried the eight dead ones that afternoon with full family honors out under the pine tree in the back yard beside the graves of the goldfish and our beloved kitten, Patches. I told them I didn't know any rituals for burying gophers but I did manage to say a prayer and then we all joined hands and sang "Amazing Grace." The kids cried, Jo shed some motherly tears, and I did my best to appear properly solemn.

When we got back into the house Jo fixed some more warm milk and took up the vigil once again with the surviving baby. He seemed to perk up, and he got stronger with every feeding. By the end of the week he had grown about an inch and he continued to grow at that rapid rate every week. By the end of the summer he was almost nine inches tall when he stood up on his hind legs — which he loved to do whenever we sat down at the table for a meal. The kids would feed him scraps from their plates. He was particularly fond of Froot Loops, peanut butter and marshmallows. He seemed to thrive on this peculiar combination, and after a while they became the only things he would eat. By October, Milton, as we called him now (after our district superintendent), for he was in every way a full member of the family, was an astounding 16 inches tall, and he had begun to fill out. He must have weighed almost four pounds. Even in their natural state gophers tend to stay long and lean, so Milton was fairly hefty for a gopher.

By Christmas time his size had doubled. Milton weighed eight pounds and he was 32 inches tall, and he was still growing. We called the zoos and they had never heard of anything like it, said it must have something to do with his diet. Milton kept eating his Froot Loops and peanut butter, but along about February or March he gave up marshmallows and his growth spurts and weight gains seemed to slow down after that. It was a good thing too; we were afraid he was going to be the fattest gopher in captivity!

I use the word captivity advisedly. Milton had the run of the house and the yard, too. We made a little swinging door in the bottom portion of the kitchen door so he could come and go as he pleased. He could have run away any time he chose, but where was he going to go, and besides he knew he had a good thing going.

Things went along very well for a couple of years. Milton was the perfect family pet. The kids taught him tricks. He could do anything a dog could do, and more. He became very good at catching the Frisbee on the fly. He got so good that we decided to enter him in a national Frisbee catching contest. It was to be held in St. Louis that year, in the park under the Arch.

There was only one hitch. When we got him down there, there was some question at first about his eligibility. The registrar said, "What kind of dog is he?" "Gopher," we said. Well, he had never heard of a gopher dog. We didn't try to explain, figured it would take too long, and who would believe us anyway? He finally agreed to let him go ahead under the category of mixed breed. We didn't see any reason to object as long as he got to compete.

Milton did exceptionally well in the preliminary rounds, but when it came time for the finals we were all beginning to have our doubts. He was up against a Whippet and a Golden Retriever. The Golden Retriever dropped his Frisbee in the first go-round, so it came down to Milton and the Whippet. The Whippet was to go first. The Frisbee was thrown out high and long. The Whippet ran out under it, jumped into the air, and did a full somersault in front of the grandstand and caught it on the way down. The judges gave him a high nine, and everybody said he would have gotten a perfect 10 if he hadn't bitten halfway through the Frisbee when he landed. Still, it was going to be a hard act to follow.

Milton looked pretty nervous. His little red sweat band was soaking wet. We told him to just go out and do his best. The Frisbee was thrown out long and high. Milton raced out, positioned himself directly beneath it, leaped into the air, turned a double somersault in front of the judges' stand, landed firmly on his feet, tossed the unmarked Frisbee to the judges, and then dipped his head to the crowd. They went wild! Milton was the Frisbee catching champion of the world. What a fuss they made over him.

When we got home the whole town turned out to welcome us. Milton got to ride on the fire truck in front of the high school band. It was an occasion none of us will ever forget.

Milton is retired from Frisbee catching now. He made enough money from personal appearances and endorsements to live very comfortably in his old age without having to work another day in his life — but he soon grew bored with the sedentary life and decided to go into public service — but that is another story.

Author's Note: *I have never told this story on a Sunday morning in worship and doubt that I ever will. It has been well received at story concerts and around the fire at the family camp.*

Reprints

The following stories are scheduled to appear in *Seasons: The Inter Faith Family Journal,* Inter-Faith Committee on the Family, Box 2018, Milwaukee, Wisconson 53201, and are reprinted here with permission.

1. "The Virgin Maude," Spring 1991.
2. "Beautiful Feet," Summer 1991.
3. "The Risen Church," Fall 1991.
4. "You Shall Receive Power," Summer 1992.
5. "Where You Do Not Wish To Go," Undated but upcoming.
6. "A Voice Crying In The Wilderness," Undated but upcoming.
7. "Love Never Ends," Undated but upcoming.
8. "The Nakedness Of Our Fathers," Undated but upcoming.
9. "I Have Seen God," Undated but upcoming.